LIBERATING INSIGHT

INTRODUCTION TO BUDDHIST PSYCHOLOGY AND INSIGHT MEDITATION

LIBERATING INSIGHT

INTRODUCTION TO BUDDHIST PSYCHOLOGY AND INSIGHT MEDITATION

By

FRITS KOSTER

Translation by

MARJÓ OOSTERHOFF

SILKWORM BOOKS

© Asoka Publishers, Rotterdam,1999
English text © Silkworm Books, 2004
Photographs © Laila Keuning
Illustrations © Fop Smit

ISBN 974- 9575-31-8

Published in 2004 by
Silkworm Books
Chiang Mai, Thailand
E-mail: silkworm@loxinfo.co.th
Website: www.silkwormbooks.info

Cover photograph © Laila Keuning
Set in 11 pt. Garamond by Silk Type
Printed by O. S. Printing House, Bangkok

05   07   09   10   08   06   04
1 3 5 7   9   8   6 4 2

CONTENTS

PART V: BUDDHISM IN THE WEST

APPENDICES

ACKNOWLEDGEMENTS

I wish to express my gratitude to Mariëtte Schoffelmeer for her critical and valuable suggestions and to Rein de Vries for his assistance with the *Satipatthāna Sutta*. I also wish to thank Carla Kamerling and Paul Boersma for their careful proof-reading; Fop Smit for his beautiful drawings as part of the meditation instructions in chapter 10; and Laila Keuning, my partner, for the final revisions, her moral support and patience, and the beautiful photographs. Finally thanks to Marjó Oosterhoff who translated the book into English, to Trasvin Jittidecharak who decided to publish the book in English, and to all those who have contributed through effort or by example to make this book possible.

I would like to dedicate the book to the Venerable P.K.K. Mettavihari, the Venerable Ajahn Asabha, to Sayadaw U Pandita and Sayadaw U Kundalābhivamsa, all of whom shared the Dhamma so generously with me and others.

May *Liberating Insight* contribute to the realisation of happiness, wisdom and inner freedom.

INTRODUCTION

For the past three decades our rapidly changing Western society has seen an increasing interest in Buddhism and in Buddhist meditation techniques. So far Tibetan and Zen Buddhism have been more popular than Theravāda Buddhism, one of the very first schools of Buddhism. Zen Buddhism became well known through advocates like the Swiss psychiatrist C. G. Jung, and because several Catholic contemplative orders integrated the practice of Zen meditation into modern Christian mysticism. Zen Buddhism also became widely known through the wonderful Japanese arts of calligraphy and haiku.

There has also been an interest in Tibetan Buddhism for some time now. This interest is due to the beautiful religious paintings, colourful culture and above all the peaceful example of the Dalai Lama, who won the Nobel Peace Prize for his non-violent resistance to the suppression of the Tibetan people and its traditions.

Theravāda Buddhism nowadays is still practised in Southeast Asia and it has only become popular in the past number of years. Some reasons for this are the increasing holiday traffic to Thailand and the brave, non-violent opposition of Aung San Suu Kyi to the military regime in Burma based on her Buddhist norms and values. But apart from this, the West is not yet very familiar with Theravāda Buddhism even though it is a profound psychology and the source from which all Buddhist schools later developed.

Liberating Insight offers a general introduction to the essence of Buddhism. It can also be viewed as a presentation of Theravāda Buddhism and its psychology of Buddhist meditation techniques, with special emphasis on the practice of insight meditation. The title of the book refers to the two fruits of this meditation practice: insight, and liberation or inner freedom.

Liberating Insight contains twenty chapters arranged in five parts. Part 1 briefly introduces the essence of Buddhism in general. It deals with the Buddha's life, the dissemination of Buddhism through the centuries and the Four Noble Truths, the quintessence of Buddhist philosophy that is common to all schools of Buddhism.

In part 2 different aspects of Buddhist ethics, like monastic rules and basic precepts for lay followers, are discussed. Concepts like karma and rebirth are also introduced. Part 2 ends with a chapter on refining ethics and the 'Four Heavenly Abodes'.

Part 3 elaborates on two different forms of meditation: tranquillity meditation, and insight or *vipassanā* meditation. The first type of meditation focusses on developing concentration so that the meditator can experience feelings of calmness and peacefulness. The goal of the second form of meditation is insight. Because the Buddha emphatically stated that this second type of meditation in particular leads to realisation of insight and inner peace, detailed instructions for its practice have been included. Part 3 ends with a chapter on the five spiritual faculties or healing powers that are developed through the practice of insight meditation.

Whereas parts 1, 2 and 3 deal with the foundations of Buddhism and meditation, part 4 is aimed at people who have practised insight meditation for some time. It consists of a description of the fruits of intensive or regular insight meditation practice. In chapter 12 various aspects of wisdom are described. Chapter 13 deals with the inner processes of purification that may result from practising insight meditation intensively, and chapter 14 continues with the experience of enlightenment as the ultimate goal of the spiritual path. The last chapter in part 4 is devoted to the obstacles encountered in meditation.

In part 5 the principles and effects of the practice of insight meditation are applied to our daily lives. Subjects of interest to our Western society have been included: health and well-being in chapter 16, the relationship between psychotherapy and meditation in chapter 17, and aspects of sexuality, relationships and communication in general in chapters 18 and 19. Part 5 closes with a chapter on stress management.

The first appendix is an English translation of the *Satipatthāna Sutta*, the Buddha's discourse on developing the four so-called foundations of mindfulness. There is also an appendix about engaged Buddhism, a glossary, a list of useful addresses and a bibliography.

Because the different chapters are interconnected, it is advisable to read the book first from beginning to end. Later on, one can go back to individual chapters to study them in more detail. The book is also useful as a reference.

There seems to be a growing need, particularly in our hectic Western society, for new insights in the area of skilfully dealing with stress, illness and psychological problems. I wrote *Liberating Insight* to bring together the immense richness and profound wisdom of the ancient and, at the same time, entirely up-to-date teachings of the Buddha. I have tried to write as much as possible in accordance with the Buddhist tradition, and to present essential aspects of Buddhist psychology, not only as an Asian cultural heritage but also to translate these for a Western society and culture. I have attempted to forge a bridge from East to West, hopefully in a format that is understandable to Western readers, without being contrary to the essence of the teachings.

Frits Koster

PART I

THE ESSENCE OF BUDDHISM

Novices near 'Mid-river Pagoda', Kyauktan, Myanmar

In part 1 of this book I will outline the general aspects of Buddhism. The first chapter describes the life of the Buddha, the founder of Buddhism. The dissemination of Buddhism throughout the ages is related in chapter 2. Chapter 3 is a description of the essence of the Buddhist teachings, including the Four Noble Truths.

I

THE LIFE OF THE BUDDHA

About 2,570 years ago a little boy was born in a family named Gotama in Lumbini Park, near Kapilavatthu, a small village in northern India (nowadays southern Nepal). The boy was called Siddhattha,[1] and he was the son of king Suddhodana and queen Māyā, rulers of the small Sākya kingdom.

At the time of his birth, an old seer predicted that the boy would possibly become somebody living a spiritual life, a religious example. Because the king preferred his son to be a suitable successor rather than a wandering ascetic, he decided to give him everything he desired, so that the prince would have no reason to be dissatisfied with life in the palace. Troubles, discomfort and worries were kept outside the palace walls as much as possible, and the young prince enjoyed an extremely luxurious and 'princely' upbringing. All his heart's desires were fulfilled. When he was sixteen years old he married the beautiful princess Yasodharā, and together they lived a happy life, without ever thinking about the less pleasant aspects of the human condition.

At a certain moment, however, there came a complete change in the prince's carefree existence. This happened when on three separate pleasure trips outside the palace he was faced with the less pleasant aspects of life. During his first outing he was confronted with an old man, who was toothless and moving with difficulty. This started a process of awakening in the young prince. He began to realise that he himself would get old too, dependent on others, without youthful beauty, with a body that was badly functioning and mental faculties that would be less sharp.

During the next trip Siddhattha saw a man who was very ill and in a lot of pain. He began to appreciate that he himself would get sick too, and that life was not just a bed of roses, but also had its share of pain and misery.

When on a third trip the young prince saw a corpse lying at the side of the road, he lost all interest in the pleasures of the palace. He hardly ate, slept badly, had nightmares and no longer enjoyed dancing, music and other forms of entertainment.

His father began to worry and organised a fourth outing, hoping that this would help his son to get over his depression. On this trip the prince, looking around without any interest in his surroundings, saw a simple ascetic who had renounced all worldly pleasures and was looking for a profound wisdom within. This man had few possessions, but radiated peace and harmony. The prince was so struck by this man's peaceful countenance that he left the palace that very night, tired and repulsed by the luxurious life he had lived until then.

At the age of twenty-nine he renounced the royal life and started to look for a deeper happiness, the happiness that comes from wisdom and insight. He began to seek ways to gain insight into the extraordinary, seemingly inevitable process of birth, old age, sickness and death.

After the *bodhisatta*[2] had given away the possessions and jewellery he had with him, and had put his hair in a topknot – which in those days was the custom for people who renounced ordinary worldly life – he decided to engage in the practice of meditation. He went to look for two of the most respected meditation teachers of that time: Ālāra Kālāma and Uddaka Rāmaputta. These teachers were instructing the practice of tranquillity or *samatha* meditation.[3] The main technique in this form of meditation is developing concentration or one-pointedness of mind, which may result in a deep mental peacefulness and happiness. The meditator focuses his or her attention and concentration on one point, excluding all other (distracting) experiences like thoughts, sounds or emotions. In this way deep and blissful levels of rapture and peacefulness or serenity can be accessed, called *jhānas* in Pali.[4] It was considered the ultimate and most important form of meditation in those days, but the young ascetic was not satisfied with the results.

Soon he had reached the same level of experience as his teachers, but in his view this method of meditation only provided *temporary* peace. There was no true liberation from afflictive emotions like desire, attachment, hatred and envy. During the periods of absorption he felt very peaceful or ecstatic, but as soon as his concentration was disturbed he experienced life once more as confusing and chaotic. Disappointed, the *bodhisatta* left his teachers and decided to continue the search for an answer to his existential questions alone. He changed his approach and decided to start living in an extreme way, submitting himself to a very austere discipline. Together with five other ascetics he fasted, drank as little as possible, tried to control his breathing, tortured himself and sometimes subjected himself to very harsh weather conditions. He practised in this way for about six years, but did not achieve the desired results. His body had become skin and bone, and the young ascetic was so weak that he had hardly enough strength to stay upright. However, he had not yet obtained liberating insight, and he still recognised all kinds of troublesome and persistent emotions in himself.

Just before he would have collapsed and died, he suddenly remembered how as a little boy – after having eaten delicious food – he had gone to sit down under a tree. In a very natural way he had watched his breathing and the processes that arose in between like thoughts, emotions, sounds and so on. He had never felt so much peace and clarity as at that time. Reflecting back on this occasion, the ascetic decided to give up his fasting and self-mortification and to try a new way to gain insight. Up until that moment he had tried two ways of dealing with physical feelings, thoughts, emotions and the like. On the one hand he knew about giving in to and indulging in all pleasurable sensual impulses. As a prince he had known this way of life. Although living like this had given him much satisfaction, it had not resulted in any insight but rather in forms of dependency, attachment, and blindness with regard to the unpleasant aspects of life.

Subsequently he had been living for six years in a very strict and rigid manner, trying to suppress or control all physical needs, thoughts and emotions. The *bodhisatta* had not realised deeper insight, peace and freedom in this way either. Besides he had physically become so weak that he could hardly continue his spiritual search.

Now the *bodhisatta* decided to follow the middle way between these two extremes. Not indulging in or chasing after physical feelings, thoughts, emotions and sensual impressions, but not suppressing or condemning these experiences either.

From that moment on he decided to eat and sleep normally (not too much, but also not too little), and to be only an observer of his bodily and mental processes, without repressing or indulging in these processes. The ascetic accepted food again, and soon he regained his strength. The five other ascetics left the *bodhisatta*, disappointed that he had given up his fast. He remained alone and when he had completely recovered his bodily strength he went to sit under a large tree, determined not to get up until he had realised the highest possible form of wisdom.

While practising meditation the young ascetic was tempted in various ways. Several alluring thoughts and emotions[5] arose in him. At first he did not know what to do about this and became confused, until he saw through the illusionary nature of the temptations and reflected on what he had determined earlier on. He pulled himself together, and with a clear, strong mind the *bodhisatta* continued to meditate. After obtaining all kinds of extraordinary psychic powers and insights, at the age of thirty-five he realised *nibbāna*, which may be translated literally as 'no longer blowing or burning' or more freely as 'enlightenment'.[6]

From that moment onwards the young prince was called *Buddha*, meaning 'woken up from ignorance'. For the remainder of his life the Buddha shared the spiritual riches he discovered with others, out of love and compassion for the suffering of humankind. According to the scriptures the Buddha was not actively proselytising, but he mainly responded to the queries and needs of the people who came to seek him out. Because of his radiant expression, sharp intelligence and unfailing intuition, the Buddha became well known and the number of students grew quickly. Soon a community of monks (and later nuns) was established for people who wanted to devote themselves to practising the *Dhamma*, the Buddha's teachings. When the Buddha died at the age of eighty-two, there was already a large community of followers: monks and nuns, and lay or non-monastic people, who had realised more happiness, wisdom and inner freedom through these teachings.

NOTES

1. The name Siddhattha (or Siddhartha in Sanskrit) means 'a wish fulfilled'.

2. In Buddhism in its more original form, a *bodhisatta* is somebody who is striving for higher wisdom and for a state of perfection or enlightenment, out of compassion for humanity. In order to realise this a *bodhisatta* is working for many lifetimes to perfect the *pāramis* or ten perfections of mind: generosity, morality, renunciation, wisdom, effort, patience, truthfulness, determination, lovingkindness and equanimity.

3. Words in italic are Pali terms. Pali is a dialect spoken at the time of the Buddha in North India. The earliest Buddhist scriptures are written in Pali. Nowadays it is a dead language, comparable to Latin in the Roman Catholic Church.

4. For more information about tranquillity meditation and the *jhānas*, see chapter 8.

5. In Buddhist texts these temptations are called *Māra*, symbolic of forms of desire, fear and other difficult emotions in us. More information about *Māra's* temptations can be found in chapter 15.

6. The experience of enlightenment can be realised by everyone. According to the scriptures, it is of great benefit because emotions like desire, hatred and ignorance – usually difficult to manage, and sometimes destructive too – are completely extinguished for that moment, purifying and liberating us. See chapters 3, 12 and 14 for a more detailed explanation of *nibbāna*.

THE DISSEMINATION OF BUDDHISM

Immediately after the Buddha died his followers organised a large gathering or council. This council was presided over by the Venerable Kassapa, and five hundred fully enlightened monks had been invited to record the teachings of the Buddha. On this occasion the Venerable Upāli recited the monastic rules and the precepts for lay followers. These have been laid down as the Vinaya.

The Venerable Ānanda, who had always been very close to the Buddha and who had looked after him, had a very sharp memory. Because of this talent of his he was asked to recite all the direct teachings of the Buddha; these have been preserved as the *suttas*. Through the work of the Venerable Sāriputta and other discerning monks, a profound treatment of Buddhist psychology evolved later, known as the *Abhidhamma* or 'Higher Teachings'.

Together these three textual bodies constitute the *Tipitaka*, literally 'the three baskets'. The Vinaya and the *suttas* were initially learned by heart in their entirety and transmitted orally; two centuries later they were inscribed on palm leaves for the first time (in Sri Lanka). All these original texts are in Pali. The Pali canon is said to contain eleven times more material than the Bible.

Two centuries after the Buddha passed away a large empire was established in India under Emperor Asoka. This emperor was initially known for his brutality and lust for power. However, when confronted with his deeds by a young monk who had a deep meditative realisation, the emperor converted to Buddhism. From that moment onwards he began to rule according to the advice of the Buddha: just, non-violent and generous. In various places in India and Nepal even now 'Asoka pillars' can be found; these are pillars inscribed with wise words of advice and decorated with one to four lion heads on top. Asoka's empire extended even as far as Iran, Turkey and Greece. In these countries there are still traces of Buddhism.

Emperor Asoka had a son called Mahinda and a daughter called Sanghamittā. They ordained as monk and nun, travelled to Sri Lanka and established Buddhism there. Furthermore Asoka sent two monks – Sona and Uttara – to Burma, from where Buddhism spread to Thailand, Laos, Cambodia and Indonesia. Monks also travelled to South China to establish Buddhism there.

Buddhism as practised in all these countries is called Theravāda Buddhism[1] and it is still flourishing today in Southeast Asia and Sri Lanka.

During the first century A.D. there was a split in the Sangha, the community of followers or practitioners of the Dhamma. A number of followers thought the Theravāda tradition too elitist and only for people who renounced the ordinary worldly life and ordained as monks or nuns. They advocated a less difficult approach where lay people would be able to experience more spiritual opportunities. This new school came to be called Mahāyāna Buddhism or 'the Great Vehicle'. New texts, insights and interpretations of existing teachings were written down in Sanskrit, and the emphasis shifted from wisdom to compassion.[2]

In this new approach the word *bodhisatta* was given a much broader interpretation. In Theravāda Buddhism a *bodhisatta* was somebody who tried to achieve a state of perfection or enlightenment, out of compassion for all human beings. Such a wish or a vow should be made in the presence of a previous Buddha.[3] According to the original scriptures the historical Buddha – Gotama Buddha – took the *bodhisatta* vow in the presence of the previous Buddha – Dipankāra Buddha. For many lifetimes he worked to perfect his *pāramis* or perfections of mind, namely generosity, virtue, renunciation, wisdom, effort, patience, truthfulness, determination, lovingkindness and equanimity. As the prince Siddhattha, whose life story has been related in the first chapter, he ultimately realised the highest state of enlightenment with the perfection of wisdom.

The title *bodhisatta* was in the Theravāda tradition only used for a Buddha who was not yet enlightened. In Mahāyāna Buddhism anybody who was determined not to reach enlightenment until all living beings have been liberated from suffering could be called a *bodhisattva*.[4] The ideal of the individual path to enlightenment was replaced in Mahāyāna Buddhism by the more accessible ideal of the *bodhisattva*.

Buddhism in East Asia in particular has been strongly influenced by Mahāyāna Buddhism. In China various Mahāyāna schools developed, among which the devotional Pure Land school and later Ch'an Buddhism with its emphasis on meditation. The founder of Ch'an was the renowned monk Bodhidharma. In the sixth century A.D. he travelled via the Silk Route from India to China and Korea. Together with the Pure Land school, Ch'an Buddhism spread from China to Japan, evolving into the well-known Zen Buddhism, with its beautiful anecdotes and extraordinary meditative arts like archery, flower arrangement and calligraphy.

About 650 years after Christ the Indian prince and monk Padmasambhava travelled from North India via Sikkim and Bhutan to Tibet. Here people practised a form of shamanic animism called Bön. Padmasambhava combined aspects and deities of the Bön culture with elements from Mahāyāna Buddhism. The result was a new school called *Vajrayāna* or 'the Diamond Vehicle', famous for its colourful *thangkas* or religious paintings, and its many forms of meditation.

This new discipline is usually called tantric or Tibetan Buddhism. From the oldest Nyingmapa tradition later on the Sakyāpa, the Gelugpa and the Kagyupa lineages evolved.

BUDDHISM IN THE WEST

Nowadays the different Buddhist schools and traditions are slowly beginning to be established in Western society. A few factors that contributed to this movement from East to West are:

- In the fifties the so-called beat generation in the U.S., with protagonists like Jack Kerouac and Alan Watts, became interested in oriental forms of spirituality.
- Because of the Chinese invasion of Tibet many Tibetan monks had to flee their country. Well-known teachers like Akong, Sogyal and Trungpa Rinpoches established themselves in the U.S. or in Europe, encountering a fertile soil for the Dhamma.
- In the sixties hippies and the 'flower power' generation became interested in Eastern mysticism, wisdom and meditation.
- Because means of mass communication are improving all the time, Western people become more and more familiar with oriental culture.
- From the seventies onwards (Jungian) psychotherapeutic schools showed an interest in the oriental view of the neurotic and healthy mind. Elements from Buddhist psychology have for instance been integrated into Gestalt and Transpersonal psychology.[5]
- In the seventies, as a reaction to the secularisation and the 'technocratification' of Western society, so-called new age movements developed. They stressed the unity and wholeness of man, nature and cosmos, and advocated an intuitive and sensitive approach to life. They emphasised non-dogmatic, individualistic spiritual practice and turned to Eastern forms of spirituality and mysticism.

- The Nobel Peace Prize given to the Dalai Lama and to Aung San Suu Kyi highlighted the peaceful Buddhist perspective on war and violence.
- During the past years Western society seems to have entered a phase of extreme complexity so rapidly that there is a growing need for simplicity and for practical, non-dogmatic ways to come home to the here and now in this busy, stressful chaos.

It is a fascinating and dynamic process, for Eastern as well as Western seekers of wisdom.

NOTES

1. Theravāda means literally 'the words or advice of the elders'. Other schools developed later from Theravāda Buddhism, which is also known as 'the Southern School'.

2. Traditional Buddhism is sometimes called Hīnayāna, 'Small' or 'Narrow Vehicle'. It needs to be pointed out, however, that wisdom and compassion are developed in both schools, and that essentially all forms of Buddhism lead to a liberated and altruistic life.

3. In Buddhist cosmology there is more than one Buddha, and it is considered a natural law that once in a number of centuries somebody realises this level, always during a time when the essence of the Buddhist teachings are in danger of falling into oblivion.

4. Bodhisattva is the more accessible equivalent of the Pali term *bodhisatta*.

5. Interesting books about the relationship between psychotherapy and Buddhim are *Thoughts without a Thinker* and *Going to Pieces without Falling Apart* by Mark Epstein (see Recommended Reading).

THE FOUR NOBLE TRUTHS

What is the essence of the Buddhist teachings? In formulating an answer to this question it is good to bear in mind that the Buddha did not intend to create a new system of dogmas or an 'ism'. He simply came to the conclusion that a certain imperfection is inherent in life. He investigated this imperfection and found a way to profound happiness and inner freedom.

The teachings of the Buddha (the Dhamma) are sometimes mistakenly called a religion, in the sense of having a theological belief system. In Buddhism the question whether or not there is a God or a higher power is not really relevant. It can, however, be called a philosophy of life. There are practical guidelines for living as well as metaphysical and mystical elements. Buddhism is one of the great faiths of the world, and it is practised mainly in Southeast Asia, China, Tibet, Korea and Japan.

The essence of Buddhism is contained in the so-called Four Noble Truths. The word 'truths' is used to indicate that it involves aspects of life that are tangible, verifiable and realistic in nature, facts in other words. The term 'noble' indicates respect for these four truths in life, and that a deep understanding of the Four Noble Truths leads to a profound and noble happiness. The Four Noble Truths are recognised by all traditions and schools of Buddhism mentioned in the previous chapter, and they are considered the foundation of the Buddhist teachings. In this chapter I will try to give a concise explanation of these four truths.

I. THE FIRST NOBLE TRUTH: THERE IS
SUFFERING (*DUKKHA SACCA*)

Whether we are young or old, born in Asia, America or in Europe, are rich or poor, Buddhist, Christian, Muslim or atheist, we are all faced to a greater or lesser degree with problems or forms of pain that are universal.

One person experiences poverty and hunger, another person is faced with (incurable) disease, and a third person may find it difficult to grow older and to cope with the physical limits it entails.

Apart from these purely physical forms of pain or discomfort we may also be confronted with mental pain. Think for instance of the burning sensation of envy or fear; feelings of frustration, unrequited love, unfulfilled desires or loneliness; disappointment because of expectations that were too high or too low; sadness caused by the loss of a loved one. These are aspects of pain all of us will encounter sooner or later.

The Buddha recognised this human vulnerability and formulated it as the first of the Four Noble Truths: 'There is suffering.' The Buddha himself used the Pali term *dukkha*. The meaning of the word *dukkha* can probably be rendered best as the unsatisfactory, unfulfilled, frustrating, conflicting and painful nature of life.

This diagnosis of the nature of life is very profound. First of all we can suffer in a direct and very obvious way. All forms of physical and mental pain, as mentioned above, are included in this. But as human beings we also experience many pleasant moments in life: being in love, sensual pleasures, feelings of peace or happiness. Although we do not immediately experience such moments as painful, in Buddhist psychology they are considered unsatisfactory, mainly because of their impermanent nature. These pleasant experiences are not everlasting and ever present; sooner or later they will disappear. The more we have become attached to these feelings, the more pain we will experience when they disappear again. Look for instance at how a small child can start to cry and protest when his or her sweets are taken away. This second type of *dukkha* is a hidden or less obvious form of suffering.

There are many experiences in life that are neither pleasant nor unpleasant but neutral in character – simple moments, perhaps, of merely seeing, hearing or thinking, unaccompanied by (strong) pleasant or unpleasant feelings. These experiences too are called unsatisfactory, because they offer no lasting peace. Besides, they are a source of suffering when we are not aware of their presence or of their neutral character. This ignorance can easily result in dullness, apathy, boredom or uncertainty. In other words, from a Buddhist point of view all worldly phenomena are ultimately unsatisfactory because of their impermanent and uncontrollable nature.

II. THE SECOND NOBLE TRUTH: THERE IS A CAUSE OF SUFFERING (*SAMUDAYA SACCA*)

Just as an illness often has a cause – whether directly or indirectly – in the same way the Buddha discovered (as the second noble truth) that the suffering we experience as human beings has a cause: desire or craving, and the attachment that often follows from this. He mentioned three obvious forms of desire and attachment.

1. Sense desire (*kāmatanhā*)

Desire, and the attachment that arises so easily from it, with regard to everything we see, hear, smell, taste or touch, the desire for (more) pleasure, luxury and comfort.

It seems that as human beings we spend a lot of our time satisfying or trying to satisfy sensual desire. Often one desire has barely been satisfied or we are attracted to another sensory stimulus that we want to run after. In advertising this is put to good use and the senses are titillated with images of beautiful men and women in exquisite clothes, with exotic make-up, strong cigarettes and so on.

The Buddha never condemned enjoying sensory desires because, whether we like it or not, it is something that potentially motivates us, something that is inherent in life. However, the Buddha did come to the conclusion that desire can be the cause of pain, sorrow, (inner) conflict and dependency, and that it can be addictive or blinding for many people. *Nearly every living being is enslaved by desire*, the Buddha declared. It limits our inner freedom; satisfaction of the senses is usually quite short-lived and therefore only provides relative happiness, particularly when we look at how much money, time and energy we sometimes invest in obtaining the desired sensual pleasures. Furthermore, sensory impulses can sometimes be present in such a dominant way that we may (unwittingly) harm ourselves and others. Sexual desire, for example, can cause all kinds of frustration and even lead to big and traumatic problems, as in the case of incest or abuse. Or we see that people who are addicted to alcohol, drugs or gambling can completely ruin themselves and others.

These are extreme forms of suffering which largely arise from sensual desire. In fact most people know one or more (less severe) kinds of addiction or sensual dependency with regard to eating, drinking, cigarettes, coffee, sugar, watching television and so on.

2. The desire to be or to become something or somebody (*bhavatanhā*, literally 'craving for existence')
This second category implies the desire to accomplish something or to be something or somebody. In fact our whole life is permeated by this lust for life and becoming. It is the energy that arouses us to satisfy basic human needs like eating, drinking, resting sufficiently, protection against heat, cold or violence, and earning enough money to be able to live.

Apart from these basic needs, this impulse is manifested as the need to prove or show ourselves in one way or another. Here are some examples: working in order to have a sense of self-worth; self-aggrandisement; the urge or ambition to get a different or better job or position; perfectionism; 'should-isms'[1]; the desire for (more) power or influence; the wish to be a father or a mother; wanting to have the last say; or to practise generosity in order to impress other people.

This second form of desire does not need to be condemned either. However, if we cannot deal with this type of craving, we easily fall (unconsciously) victim to this impulse, and this can result in stress, inner tension and psychosomatic problems. In more extreme cases it may cause a nervous breakdown, symptoms of burnout, suppression, or ethically irresponsible behaviour in our relationships with others. Being ambitious seldom leads to real forms of happiness and harmony, and causes inner unrest time and time again. Besides, this running after ambitions often happens to the detriment of our own mental and physical well-being and that of others.

3. The desire to destroy (*vibhavatanhā*)

This desire, too, is deeply rooted in our lives, and is manifested as the desire not (or no longer) wanting to have or to be something. Examples of these forms of desire are not (or no longer) accepting physical discomfort, pain, illness, thoughts, sorrow, anger and other human experiences. This impulse can also show itself in acting from a negative self-image or wanting to end or lose something we obtained at an earlier time; it may cause (inner) conflicts, resignation from work, break-up of a relationship, even war or the killing of ourselves and/or others. The first two forms of desire are strong forces sucking us in or overpowering us, whereas the third desire is repulsive in nature and synonymous with hatred or aversion.

In Buddhism the three types of desire are said to be the *immediate* cause of pain and sorrow, in particular when we cannot deal skilfully with these impulses. But Buddhist psychology mentions a *deeper* or underlying cause of human suffering that prevents us coping adequately with these driving forces. This fundamental cause is rooted in ignorance (*avijjā*), not understanding or misunderstanding reality. This ignorance is not at all a lack of intellectual knowledge; it is not being (clearly) aware of or interpreting unwisely[2] sensory input and mental and physical experiences the moment they arise.

This subtle delusion is not as clearly recognisable, but it creates various problems behind the scenes. Because of *avijjā* we do not know or are unclear about what is happening here and now. This causes us to deal unskilfully with desires, attachments or conflicts.

A good simile is a house with six doors. In moments of unawareness and unmindfulness, a burglar can easily enter the house and do damage. But if there is a guard, who keeps an eye on the six doors, he can see or notice when someone wants to enter. The intruder will cause less damage or none at all. In this analogy the house represents the six human senses, namely ears, eyes, nose, tongue, body and mind.

In Buddhist psychology it is said that ultimately all problems arise from ignorance. Not being aware and being blinded in relation to pleasant impulses result in desire and attachment. With unpleasant impulses they cause aversion, hatred, fear or jealousy, and with neutral impulses they lead to confusion, uncertainty, boredom or apathy. In this way we as human beings create unconsciously or only half consciously all kinds of patterns in our thinking and acting that keep us in bondage and cause suffering. We may be searching all our lives for a mirage or a castle in the air; we can see it, but it is always just out of reach.

III. THE FOURTH NOBLE TRUTH: THERE IS A WAY THAT LEADS TO THE ENDING OF SUFFERING (*MAGGA SACCA*)

It is intentional that for the time being I skip the third noble truth, because in my view it can best be explained by means of the fourth

noble truth. The fourth noble truth can be seen as a guide to
Dhamma practice, and it is usually called the Eightfold Path. This
path can be compared to a homeopathic remedy that is made up
of eight ingredients or guidelines on how to live one's life. Together these eight guidelines constitute the fourth noble truth: the
way that leads to the end of suffering. There are various levels to
the practice of the Eightfold Path. First of all the Eightfold Path is
diagnostic in nature (as regards the illness or the problem).
Futhermore, it can lead to quicker and better acceptance of the
difficulties and limitations. It also has a healing effect in the sense
that following the Eightfold Path can result in alleviating human
suffering, and eventually lead to the complete ending of suffering.
In this chapter I have opted to reflect only briefly on the eight
guidelines of the Eightfold Path.

1. RIGHT UNDERSTANDING (*sammā ditthi*). This means
   the discernment or wisdom that allows us to find a way that
   leads to more happiness, insight and harmony. From this
   basic insight we walk a spiritual path whereby thoughts are
   developed or directed in a wise(r) manner.

2. RIGHT THOUGHT (*sammā sankappa*). In Buddhist texts
   we are advised to nourish or reinforce three types of thoughts
   without, however, ignoring or suppressing the opposite types
   of thoughts. These three kinds of thoughts are:
   • thoughts renouncing (sensual) desire and attachment
   • thoughts not rooted in hatred or anger
   • thoughts that are free from resentment

A simple example of developing right thought is planning to
smoke less when you notice that smoking affects you badly. Other
examples are seeing the good in people, being open to the suffering of others, and practising meditation on lovingkindness.[3]

The first two guidelines of the Eightfold Path are aspects of wisdom (*pañña*); the next three guidelines are connected with ethical behaviour or morality (*sila*).

3. RIGHT SPEECH (*sammā vācā*). The advice connected with right speech is to refrain from telling lies, from gossiping, cursing or talking nonsense, particularly when this may cause unnecessary confusion, pain or sorrow,

4. RIGHT ACTION (*sammā kammanta*). This fourth guideline of the Eightfold Path is the advice to refrain from actions that cause disharmony and are (self-) destructive. Examples are killing, stealing, violent or abusive sexual conduct, and using alcohol or drugs (to the degree that it affects our clarity of mind).

5. RIGHT LIVELIHOOD (*sammā ājiva*). Just like the two previous guidelines, right livelihood is another guideline to refrain from hurting ourselves and others in our jobs, hobbies or other day-to-day activities. Examples are selling weapons, dealing in drugs, committing fraud or having a job that involves killing.

The last three guidelines of the Eightfold Path – largely developed through meditation – relate to how we deal with actions, thoughts and emotions on an inner level.

6. RIGHT EFFORT (*sammā vāyāma*). Right effort means the balanced effort not to provide fuel for unwholesome or unskilful thoughts and emotions, and to stop them. Furthermore, we develop and nourish wholesome deeds and emotions.

7. RIGHT MINDFULNESS (*sammā sati*). This is the power of observation with regard to what is happening in or around us in the present moment. It is an open and attentive awareness of body, feelings, thoughts, sensory impressions and emotions in the here and now.

8. RIGHT CONCENTRATION (*sammā samādhi*). The eighth and last guideline of the Eightfold Path is one-pointedness of mind.

When we look at the description of the Eightfold Path we see that the word *right* keeps recurring. Right (or correct) means in accordance with the aim of following the Eightfold Path, namely developing wisdom and harmony, and ending our suffering. It indicates a balance or (meditative) equilibrium. If we develop the sixth or the eighth guideline of the Eightfold Path too much or too little, other guidelines may be (temporarily) blocked.[4] The eight guidelines or steps of the path are connected, and they act like an upward spiral: the development of one guideline promotes the next one.

IV. THE THIRD NOBLE TRUTH: THE TRUTH OF THE ENDING OF SUFFERING (*NIRODHA SACCA*)

The Buddha once said, *Oh monks, I only teach one thing: suffering and the ending of suffering.* According to the early Buddhist scriptures, walking the Eightfold Path – condensed as the path of virtue, meditation and wisdom – leads to harmony and insight. This insight culminates in the realisation of the third noble truth: the truth of the eradication or ending of suffering. In Pali the word used in this context is *nirodha*, which can be translated as 'not being in bondage, or no longer being in bondage'.

When meditative insight is profound enough, and when the

meditator and the situation are ready, a specific and purifying experience may happen which is called 'enlightenment'.[5] This experience bears no relation to any worldly experience and therefore cannot be described. Dr. Walpola Rahula in his book *What The Buddha Taught* uses the beautiful example of a tortoise who is telling his friend (a fish) about the nice walk he took over land to get back to the sea. 'Of course', the fish replies, 'but you mean you were swimming.' The tortoise is trying to explain that you cannot swim on land, that it is solid and that you have to walk on it. But the fish maintains that this is impossible, that everything is fluid and that one can only swim or dive. Likewise it is nearly impossible to explain exactly what mangoes taste like to somebody who has never eaten mangoes.

In Buddhist texts the experience of enlightenment is often described by way of negations, explaining what it is *not*. It *is* described generally as 'a state of highest bliss and peace'(*santi*), because it is disconnected from all (impermanent) worldly experience; as 'safe' (*khema*); as 'liberating' (*vimutti*).

This enlightenment experience is not lasting. It can be compared to getting a glimpse of the sun on a cloudy day. According to the Buddha and to meditators who have had this experience, it is extremely liberating, because for that moment previous blockages and troublesome forces like desire, hatred and ignorance, are completely extinguished.[6]

The Eightfold Path may be seen as the practical way and the process of awakening that leads to the realisation of the *summum bonum* of the Buddhist teachings.

It needs to be pointed out, however, that walking this Eightfold Path also bears many fruits in the short or long term *without* realising the transcendental experience referred to above. I will discuss this in detail in chapters 12, 13 and 14.

In Buddhism walking or practising the Eightfold Path has been compared to a lotus. These plants have their roots in the dark, muddy bottom of the pond; this is their feeding ground. In the same way our spiritual journey starts in the mud of unawareness, confusion, pain and suffering. By becoming mindful of this in a non-judgmental way, slowly but surely a beautiful, radiant flower grows; the flower of purity, compassion and wisdom.

The Eightfold Path leading to the ending of suffering can be divided into three main themes, namely ethical or moral conduct (*sila*), meditation (*samādhi*), and wisdom or insight (*paññā*). Because these three themes have a very important and purifying function according to Buddhist psychology, I would like to develop these main themes in parts 2, 3 and 4 of this book.

NOTES

1. 'Should', 'must', 'should have' and 'ought to' are words indicating the presence of (sometimes unreasonably high) demands we place on ourselves and others.

2. In some situations we can be clearly aware of the unwholesome effects of an action, but nevertheless we cannot refrain from doing this action, even against our better judgement.

3. This type of meditation and mental development will be explained in chapter 7.

4. More explanation about this can be found in chapter 15 in the section 'Māra's fifth army'.

5. In Pali this experience is called *nibbāna*; the Sanskrit equivalent is *nirvāna*.

6. More will be said in chapter 14 about this liberating experience.

PART II

ETHICS

The wheel of rebirth, painted by an unknown artist,
© Maitreya Institute, Emst, the Netherlands

Part 2 of this book deals with ethics or moral conduct. In the fourth chapter I will give an introduction to the term ethics from a Buddhist point of view. Chapter 5 will introduce the term karma, the law of cause and effect, which is closely connected with ethical norms and values. In chapter 6 I consider the meaning of 'rebirth', in light of the law of karma. Part 2 concludes with a chapter about 'refined' ethics. As a practical example of this I will describe the four so-called Sublime Mental States, and give some examples of how these mind states can be developed.

4

ETHICS IN BUDDHISM

Ethics may be described as a set of rules or guidelines for conduct, based on values and concepts about what is wholesome and what is not. Just as in any other philosophy, in Buddhism ample attention is given to ethics or *sila* in Pali. A large part of the Buddhist scriptures concerns moral conduct or ethics. The third, fourth and fifth guidelines of the Eightfold Path – right speech, right action and right livelihood – involve ethical activities, and form an important foundation of this spiritual path.

For us westerners (with a Christian background) the concept of ethics or morality sometimes causes resistance. This is because norms and values are often laid down as dogmas, unconsciously creating a sense of loss of inner freedom. Therefore I prefer to describe the ethics used in Buddhism as a voluntary code of conduct, not based on dogma.

Perhaps this non-dogmatic aspect of ethics is most clearly indicated by the Buddha's advice to a group of confused Kālāmas, inhabitants of the town of Kesaputta.

> Do not be led by reports, tradition or hearsay. Do not be led by the authority of religious texts, nor by mere logic or inference; nor by considering appearances, nor by delight in speculations; nor by seeming possibilities, nor by the idea 'this is our teacher'. But, Kālāmas, when you know for yourselves that certain things are unwholesome, are wrong and bad, then give them up . . . and when you know for yourselves that certain things are wholesome and good, then accept and follow them.

As regards values it can be said that from a Buddhist perspective much emphasis is placed on creating harmony and peace. Behaviour that promotes harmony and peace is called wholesome; when certain behaviour is directly or indirectly causing harm or pain to ourselves and others, it is called unwholesome. Such an ethical code of conduct has many advantages:

- We live and die peacefully, without confusion or remorse.
- Morally pure behaviour causes diligence, and diligence causes mental and material well-being.
- This results in a good and respected reputation.
- We suffer less from restricting emotions like fear, remorse or doubt in initiating and maintaining social contacts.
- A code of behaviour as outlined above can provide a sound foundation for a balanced practice, without being hindered by the consequences of ethical mistakes.

A large part of the Buddhist scriptures concerns morality or virtue, where the Buddha distinguishes between monks, nuns and the laity. Monks (*bhikkhus*) are celibate and should conform to 227 precepts. These guidelines or precepts are recited every full moon and new moon day. They provide a framework for living with other monks in a simple and harmonious way, in the use of robes and other possessions, and in communicating with the laity. Monastic life is considered a fertile soil for Dhamma practice.

In the beginning of the Buddhist era there was also an order of nuns (*bhikkhunis*). Nuns were expected to follow even more precepts. Some of these precepts were laid down for their protection (living alone as a woman in the forest was dangerous); other precepts were the product of patriarchal Indian society. Although the Buddha did state clearly that women have equal spiritual potential – and there are many stories about enlightened women – he could not (or did not dare to) change the deeply rooted male-oriented cultural structures into a monastic form that was the same for monks and nuns.

Because monastic life was so much more difficult for nuns than for monks, the original nuns' order disappeared for a considerable time and was replaced with an order of nuns observing ten precepts.[1] The same precepts are observed by novice monks (*sāmaneras*).

All precepts follow from five basic precepts or guidelines with regard to moral conduct for lay people. This advice or these guidelines are based on the view that distinction can be made between what is wholesome and conducive to harmony, and what is not. These precepts are:

- The advice not to kill.
- The advice not to steal.
- The advice not to behave sexually in ways that are violent, disruptive and abusive. (From this point of view unsolicited or unwanted sexual intimacy is harmful, but homosexuality is not necessarily so.)
- The advice not to tell lies, not to gossip or curse.
- The advice not to use alcohol and drugs to the extent that our minds get clouded and we harm ourselves or others physically, mentally, emotionally or socially.

It is difficult to judge a verbal or physical action as such on its wholesome or unwholesome qualities. The determining factor in wholesomeness is mainly the intention or the motivation from which we act. When our motivation is coloured by desire, hatred and/or ignorance, then – from a Buddhist perspective – the action is considered unwholesome. When our motivation is not coloured by these three driving forces, it is considered wholesome action. For instance we might tell (white) lies in order to prevent direct or indirect harm. We may also talk about somebody, not to gossip but to gain insight into the behavioural patterns of that person.

Ultimately concrete advice about ethically responsible behaviour cannot be got from a book. Therefore it is best to view the Buddhist code of conduct as a framework or guide that enables us to live harmoniously, and not to see it as a straitjacket. For every precept we could think of an example where this precept is inadequate and where it is difficult to make a decision. This is why in Buddhism guidelines are given rather than prohibitions or commandments, giving us the freedom to make our own choices. We can break as many precepts as we want, as it were. However, we ourselves will (most likely) suffer the consequences too. In this connection I think it will clarify matters to introduce the concept of karma, which I will do in the next chapter.

NOTES

1. Recently it has become possible for women in some Asian countries (and in the West) to get full ordination as a *bhikkhuni* and to observe the traditional 311 precepts for *bhikkhuni*. We see that the women's liberation movement of the West is slowly gaining momentum in Asia.

5

KARMA

Nowadays the term karma – originally an oriental concept – becomes more and more incorporated into the English language, and it is widely used in 'new age' circles.

In fact it is a very old concept. In ancient Indian pre-Buddhist philosophy, karma was often viewed as 'fate' or a course of life that was more or less fixed, conditioned by the past. It was seen as something static, with fatalistic connotations. The Indian caste system is based on it. The Buddha grew up with this concept, but as a philosopher and teacher he made some radical changes. This chapter is mainly intended to clarify the concept of karma from a Buddhist perspective.

First of all let us examine the word 'karma'. It is a Sanskrit term and means literally 'deed' or 'action'. In Buddhism this means all physical, verbal and mental activities that are done knowingly and intentionally. Hence all our involuntary, unconscious and/or unintended actions are not considered karma. For instance when we unintentionally crush an ant, this is not a karmically loaded action; if we do it on purpose, then it is.

In Buddhist philosophy there is no higher power that forces us do things or to which we are accountable. So we need not be afraid of the judgement of a higher power, but we can of course let others influence us. Our actions under the influence of others are karmically less powerful, and the result or the fruit (*vipāka*) will consequently be less sweet or bitter.

Likewise we are not determined by a 'self' or soul; according to the *Abhidhamma* (the 'Higher Teachings' or Buddhist psychology) there is merely a process of cause and effect of physical and mental phenomena, conditioned by motives and habitual patterns. This principle endows us with an extreme responsibility for our own actions. Even though we can indeed be influenced by others, ultimately we ourselves are responsible.

Before karma (or *kamma* in Pali) takes place there are impulses or driving forces: generators that make the engine run. Six of these driving forces or *hetus* are mentioned, namely desire, hatred, ignorance (lack of a sense of reality), and the absence of any of these three. The first three driving forces or roots are inherent in unwholesome karma; the last three are connected with wholesome karma.

Desire and hatred are not forbidden or sinful emotions; it is merely pointed out that these emotions directly or indirectly cause harm or pain when we do not deal with them wisely. In Buddhism there is no such thing as 'having lost face forever'. Nor is there the concept of '(eternal) sin'. Mistakes and oversights arise from ignorance; something was not known, not understood correctly, or interpreted incorrectly at the time.

As regards the last three roots, it needs to be mentioned that just the absence of desire, hatred and ignorance is already seen as wholesome, and that their opposites (generosity, lovingkindness and wisdom) involve stronger qualities of wholesome karma.

In Buddhist texts ten clearly recognisable forms of wholesome and unwholesome karma are mentioned, originating from the six impulses or roots.

Wholesome (*kusala*) karma:
1. Practising generosity
2. Observing an ethical code of conduct that promotes harmony (see the previous chapter)
3. Practising meditation
4. Treating ourselves and others with respect
5. Being of service, and being altruistic

6. Sharing merit with others
7. Rejoicing in the happiness and prosperity of others
8. Reading about, listening to and talking about subjects that foster harmony and awareness
9. Explaining the Dhamma
10. Correcting our own blind spots

Unwholesome (*akusala*) karma:
1. Killing
2. Stealing
3. Sexual misconduct (in the sense of harming)
4. Telling lies
5. Gossiping
6. (Inappropriate) use of crude language, cursing
7. Talking nonsense
8. Greed
9. Ill will
10. Having a wrong view of reality

As already stressed in the previous chapter, it is difficult to decide on the quality of karma by just looking at the action. Ultimately the motivation or the intention behind an act is determining the wholesome or unwholesome nature of an activity. A white lie, or frivolous talk to put someone at ease, is not seen as unwholesome. The result or the fruit of our actions is usually sweet if the motivation is karmically wholesome, and bitter if it is unwholesome.

This principle makes it very difficult if not impossible to judge somebody else's moral behaviour. Particularly in complex ethical issues, motives may not be clear-cut or outsiders can interpret the intentions in different ways. The law of karma clearly appeals to our faculty for introspection and mindfulness. We ourselves are best able to (learn to) understand our own true motives, and to distinguish what is conducive to harmony and what is not.

6

REBIRTH

'Rebirth' is often talked about in connection with 'the law of karma'. The principle of karma works like a continuation of energy, perpetuating what is sometimes called 'the cycle of rebirth' (*samsāra*), or freely translated as 'the merry-go-round'. It is assumed that we are not born as a *tabula rasa*, an empty slate, but that there is a psychological store of experiences and conditionings from previous lives. Likewise this life does not end completely at death, but according to the Buddha and others who have developed a deeper vision on what it means to be a human being, some kind of transfer of energy takes place.

The principle of rebirth can be explained with a physics experiment from secondary school: five or six metal balls are suspended on a thread next to each other. When we take the ball on the extreme left, move it to the left and release it, it will hit the second ball in the row and then stop completely. The ball on the extreme right will swing to the right, as a result of the transfer or continuation of energy. We cannot see this energy and it does not have any fixed or solid shape or form; however, it is a natural law.

The ball on the extreme left can be compared to an action or to our life here and now; the stopping of the ball can be compared to the end of the action or to death. The ball on the extreme right is the result in this or in a future life. The wholesome and unwholesome motives behind the actions and experiences, together with delusion and blindness, determine the tone of the karmic energy, and thereby the nature of rebirth into the next life.

This process should not be confused with the concept of 'reincarnation', which literally means 'coming into flesh again'. This often implies a solid entity, a soul (*attā* or *atman*) which is permanent and which reunites after death with a living being. The traditional Indian caste system is based on this principle of reincarnation. Different strata of the population have their own soul or entity; someone from a lower caste can never experience a higher reincarnation. From this perspective everything is more or less predetermined.

In Theravāda Buddhism the term rebirth is preferred. There is no premise of a solid entity or soul, but rather of karmic energy that 'reproduces itself'. All (wholesome and unwholesome) motives behind our actions constitute a certain formless energy. This energy is not static or permanent, but can take on a different tone in every lifetime or rather in every moment.

Strong (pleasant, wholesome, unwholesome and sometimes traumatic) experiences and motives naturally have great impact because consciously or unconsciously we remain preoccupied with them. According to the *Abhidhamma*, experiences just before we die can have great impact on the nature of rebirth as well. Ultimately however, the broader picture of our life will show itself again and again. In other words, sooner or later we will reap what we sow now or have sown in the past. The phenomenon of rebirth can be approached in two ways.

A LITERAL INTERPRETATION OF REBIRTH

The first approach is literal and also involves – apart from this life – lives before and after this lifetime. Buddhist psychology speaks of a metaphysical system of different realms, some of which are clearly visible and others that cannot be perceived by (most) people. When the karmic tendency is generally wholesome, rebirth will take place in a comfortable or blissful realm. When the tendency is unwholesome, rebirth will take place in a less favourable realm and involve more suffering.

In this metaphysical approach rebirth can take place in six different realms (*loka*) or planes of consciousness:

- In an invisible hell, as the result of strong feelings of hatred.
- In the animal realm, as the result of fear and ignorance.
- In the realm of the 'hungry ghosts' or *peta*,[1] through obsessive (unsatisfied) desires.
- In the human realm, as the result of right ethical behaviour and understanding.
- In the realm of divine, heavenly beings or *deva*, as the result of practising generosity, lovingkindness, meditation and other wholesome actions. It is a blissful realm, with sensual pleasures, and a peaceful mind developed through concentration.
- The last of the six realms is called the realm of 'jealous demigods' or *asura*, beings who were previously *deva*, but who became jealous of the (slightly greater or different) happiness of other gods, and who therefore have fallen painfully. The result is that their existence is less blissful than that of *deva*.

For (most) people only the animal and human realms are clearly visible. However, in Buddhist scriptures there are many stories about the other four realms, describing in colourful language different cultures and characteristics, like climate, forms of pain and suffering (in the hellish realms) or different forms of pleasure (in the heavenly realms).

According to the Buddhist texts, all these planes of consciousness are – like human existence – temporary in nature. In one realm the life span might be longer than in another, but all these realms are impermanent and therefore ultimately unsatisfactory. In Buddhism human existence is viewed as the most valuable, because human beings know both pain and pleasure, so they can easily develop wisdom. In the hellish realms or in the realm of the hungry ghosts, there is apparently too much pain and misery to be able to observe one's situation calmly. Animals do not have freedom of choice and can only act and react instinctively. Heavenly beings or *deva* are so involved in their pleasures that they forget to meditate and develop wisdom. This is why our existence as a human being is rated so highly.

A FIGURATIVE INTERPRETATION

Perhaps we find it difficult to accept this interpretation. I myself also have some reservations and unanswered questions in the area of rebirth. During meditation for example, I have had dreamlike images that I could interpret as experiences from previous lives. But these images could just as easily have arisen from a vivid imagination or from watching television. To the question about what exactly will happen after death I cannot give a definitive answer either, because I lack insight and conscious memory. In any case, I think the theory of rebirth and the transmission of karmic energy is quite logical and consistent. However, I cannot speak from my own experience, and I hope to get more insight into these matters when I die.

From a more pragmatic perspective there is another interpretation of the phenomenon of rebirth that can be more easily observed and which involves this life. In this approach the six realms are seen as human mind states that can be experienced in everyday life. Sometimes we feel as if we are burning in hell, like when we are tortured in a war or burning with lovesickness. The feeling of a drug addict who cannot get his drugs in time, or the frustration we feel when we cannot get what we want, are examples of the mind state of a hungry ghost. The moment we act or react from mere instinct (through fear, hatred or the urge to survive) we live on the animal level. When we enjoy something and everything is going right for us, we experience a heavenly or divine state of mind, and when we are pained by jealousy, we live like a jealous demigod.

In this figurative or interpersonal description we experience human consciousness in those moments we are aware or conscious of our situation, so that we can make free and wise choices in life. Most people rarely experience such moments. We live mainly on the level of animals or hungry ghosts, we experience (hellish) pain and sorrow, or become totally absorbed in sensual pleasures, without any mindfulness.

From a Buddhist perspective, we can use our human existence and consciousness well. It offers the best opportunity to develop liberating insight, and to break free from the conditioning 'merry-go-round' that revolves perpetually.

NOTES

1. 'Hungry ghosts' or *peta* are described as invisible beings with a very small mouth and a narrow neck, and a very big, hollow belly. These beings are always hungry, and can never eat enough to fill their hollow bellies.

7

FOUR SUBLIME MENTAL STATES

In Buddhist psychology two kinds of ethics are distinguished, namely elementary ethics (*vāritta sila*) and refined or elaborated ethics (*cāritta sila*).

Elementary ethics involves the renunciation or restraint that is incorporated in the third, fourth and fifth guidelines of the Eightfold Path and in the five moral training precepts.[1] They are the most basic guidelines for walking the spiritual path in a harmonious way.

By refined or elaborated ethics is meant first of all the ethics of monks and nuns, where the precepts are stricter and intended to promote simplicity. Living as a monk or a nun can create many favourable circumstances or conditions, like being able to concentrate easily and quickly, having few desires, wasting little time, and having more tolerance and forbearance in dealing with discomfort and difficulties.

Some Buddhist monks and nuns hone their precepts even more by observing one or more ascetic practices (*dhutanga*). In the *Visuddhimagga*[2] thirteen of these ascetic practices are mentioned. Some monks or nuns train themselves to eat only one meal a day, for example. Others vow not to sleep in a house or under a roof, and there are even monks who never lie down but spend the whole night in meditation while sitting, standing or walking. It is said that Bhikkhu Mahā Kassapa, a disciple of the Buddha, trained himself in almost every *dhutanga* to a high degree of proficiency.

It is however not my intention to encourage anybody to start practising these austerities straightaway. If we have a family, or a busy and demanding job, I think it would not be realistic to sleep outside in the cold or eat only one meal a day. There is no point in forcing ourselves by living according to a strict discipline. These ascetic practices can also be applied in a simple manner, for instance by giving up or being more moderate in the use of cigarettes, sweets, coffee, and/or by spending less time watching television. But it is necessary to have the motivation to tighten our discipline. This motivation may be cultivated by realising or reflecting that in this way we can spend more time and money on what we consider important, and that we can develop a greater sense of freedom, independence and self-worth.

These aspects of elaborated ethics initially have an individual effect. There are also ways to practise morality where the effects are more obvious on a social level. I am referring to developing the wholesome activities and ways of behaviour as mentioned in chapter 5 (the ten wholesome forms of karma).

These wholesome activities are based on the presence of four 'friends', also called sublime mental states or (*brahmavihāra*, literally 'heavenly abodes') and they contribute to greater harmony in society:

1. Lovingkindness (*mettā*)
2. Compassion (*karunā*)
3. Sympathetic joy (*muditā*)
4. Equanimity (*upekkhā*)

In developing these four *brahmavihāra* we make no distinction between ourselves and others. These mind states are radiated to all living beings, without preference or aversion. Because these four mental powers have great healing potential, and can contribute to more inner and social happiness, I will discuss them one by one.

1. LOVINGKINDNESS

In the *Visuddhimagga* and in other scriptures the four *brahma-vihāra* and their practice are described very clearly. The Pali term mettā, usually translated as 'lovingkindness', is defined according to characteristic, function and manifestation.

Mettā has the characteristic of not being resentful and – in an active sense – promoting the well-being of ourselves and others. The function of *mettā* is to put irritation aside, and to choose for and to be involved in our own well-being and that of others. It is manifested as warmth, as a helpful and willing attitude, and as loveliness.

In this world hatred is never appeased by hatred, it is only appeased by love. This is an eternal law, states the fifth verse of the *Dhamma-pada*, a well-known Buddhist text with wise words and sayings. *Mettā* refers to gentleness and kindness. It is open and unlimited, and does not expect anything in return. It is the antithesis of hatred.

Practising lovingkindness may degenerate into attachment or sentimentality. The direct or proximate cause of *mettā* is seeing the good in ourselves and/or in others.

EXERCISE: LOVINGKINDNESS

Sit in a comfortable manner, close your eyes and wish yourself all kinds of pleasant things: 'May I be happy, free from pain, danger, hunger and thirst; may I be free from sorrow, fear, and other forms of pain or frustration.'

You can use these words or – if you prefer – choose phrases that come up in the moment, and repeat these in a calm, relaxed way. If resistance or distracting thoughts come up, note these, but at the same time continue the exercise.

After some minutes you do the same with somebody you respect or love very much, someone we might call a benefactor.[3] Next you send kind thoughts to your friends, relatives and colleagues, then to the people you only know superficially (the shopkeeper, the neighbours and so on), and then to all the people in your town or village. Then you extend the circle and let your thoughts of kindness radiate to all the people in your county/state, then to your fellow countrymen, to all those who live in the same continent as you, and finally to all the people in the whole world.

You can also incorporate animals into the practice, and if you believe in them you can also send thoughts of lovingkindness to invisible beings in blissful and/or miserable realms or mental states. Finally you can conclude the practice with a comprehensive wish like: 'May I and all other living beings be happy, free from pain, resentment and danger. May all living beings be free from suffering and live in peace and harmony.'
Remain seated quietly for a minute or so, and slowly return to the present.

This is only one of many ways in which we can develop *mettā*. Lovingkindness meditation always starts with ourselves, because it is said that we cannot truly have unconditional love if we cannot have *mettā* for ourselves. From this basis *mettā* is radiated (in ever-increasing circles) to our surroundings. The whole universe is bathed in lovingkindness and goodwill. In the texts eleven benefits of *mettā* are mentioned:

1. We can sleep well.
2. We wake up peacefully.
3. We have pleasant dreams
4. As a result of *mettā* we are automatically loved by ourselves and by others.
5. We are loved by beings in invisible realms of existence, and by animals.
6. We are protected by heavenly beings or *devas*.
7. Lovingkindness offers protection against dangers like poison, weapons, fire, fear or aggression.
8. Our face becomes radiant.
9. Our mind becomes peaceful.
10. We live and die without confusion.
11. According to the scriptures we will be reborn in blissful realms.

When we apply this traditional list of benefits to our Western society, we can see that developing lovingkindness has the following wholesome effects:

- Lovingkindness leads to greater relaxation, being able to deal better with sources of stress,[4] and to the healing of stress-related complaints.
- It results in better social skills and in higher emotional intelligence.
- Developing lovingkindness results in a stronger sense of basic

security and self-acceptance. Particularly in Western society, where many people suffer from low self-esteem, *mettā* can have a valuable healing influence on this 'disease'.
- We gain peace of mind, and thereby greater creativity.
- We are less ruled by feelings of hatred and fear.
- Lovingkindness can function as a solid foundation for the practice of insight meditation. An explanation of this form of meditation will follow in chapters 9 and 10.

2. COMPASSION

Developing compassion (*karunā*) can be very beneficial and of great significance when we need to deal with pain and disappointments in ourselves, as well as when we have to cope with the suffering of others. It is the wish to alleviate or end suffering. Compassion is the direct or immediate antithesis of cruelty or treachery. In the development of compassion, we can fall into the trap of pity when we are overwhelmed by sadness.

Compassion is a remedy for cruelty. In society it will result in a greater capacity for empathy, social responsibility and selfless service.

3. SYMPATHETIC JOY

Sympathetic joy can be seen as the wholesome opposite of jealousy. When somebody is tortured by jealousy on a regular basis, this tendency can gradually be inclined in the direction of a (spontaneous) feeling of sympathetic joy by developing *mudită*. It is not only a feeling of joy or happiness; rather it shows itself as the expression of joyful sympathy with the material or immaterial success or wealth of others. *Mudită* is congratulatory in nature, and it transcends aversion.

4. EQUANIMITY

Equanimity (*upekkhā*) – the last of the four sublime states of mind – can be seen as a stabilising force. We are able to see or judge people and situations appropriately, with balanced and discriminating wisdom, without being blinded by attachment or aversion. Equanimity is impartial in nature. It views the loved and the unloved, the pleasant and the painful, the fortunate and the unfortunate, the wholesome and the unwholesome in living beings and in circumstances from an equanimous point of view. *Upekkhā* is the remedy for (extreme) passions and feelings of hatred, and should not be confused with indifference, which is unconscious and dull in nature.

While lovingkindness, compassion and sympathetic joy obviously have an aspect of being involved and connected, equanimity transcends this involvement. This can be very liberating, particularly in situations where we cannot or do not want to act.

The four sublime states of mind or noble abodes are sometimes called 'unlimited' or *appamaññā*, because they involve the whole universe. In order to understand them, in Buddhist psychology a beautiful comparison is made of a mother with four children. Her wish for a good education and upbringing for her youngest child is the equivalent of *mettā*. Her second child is ill, and her wish for the child to get better is the manifestation of *karunā*. At the moment all is going well for her third child; her joy in this and her wish for it to continue is *muditā*. The oldest child is independent and doing well. She knows he is going his own way, and she does not need to concern herself with him.

All these four mental states can be developed as specific meditations and they promote harmony in ourselves and in society.[5] Besides being developed through formal meditation, the four *brahmavihāra* can also be cultivated in a simple way in daily life. Some examples:

- When saying goodbye or when meeting or passing somebody in the street, make the mental wish that he or she may be happy.
- Before or after a meal mentally give thanks to the people who have helped to provide your food.
- Do service or social work, help friends or relatives.
- Support a good cause.
- Pay compliments to colleagues and friends; practise living kindness.
- Do no hesitate to congratulate people with their success or good fortune.
- When you have a certain aversion to somebody's behaviour, reflect on the fact that he or she will ultimately suffer most, and that they will bear the consequences of their unwholesome behaviour.
- When you have the tendency to take on too much responsibility for things, reflect every so often that you are not responsible for all mistakes and breakdown in communication in an organisation. Imperfection is part of life.

There are various simple ways to practise the *brahmavihāra*, thereby beautifying the world. When we wish to cultivate one or all of the *brahmavihāra* more intensively, it is recommended to read about the subject, and to choose a suitable practice, if possible under the guidance of a teacher or expert in this field. *Lovingkindness* is the title of a book with clear explanations and many practical (meditation) exercises with regard to the *brahmavihāra*, written by Sharon Salzberg, an American meditation teacher. She is a very experienced practitioner of these four sublime states of mind.

We will notice that developing the four *brahmavihāra* and integrating them into our activites, gives satisfaction and a deeper meaning to our lives. It is a skilful way to transform troublesome or persistent tendencies into forces that promote harmony and well-being.

NOTES

1. See chapters 3 and 4.

2. This book was written about four hundred years after Christ by a Sinhalese monk, the Venerable Buddhaghosa. It was translated into English by Bhikkhu Ñānamoli as *The Path of Purification*. It is one of the most comprehensive manuals of Buddhist meditation.

3. Initially, it is preferable that this not be your lover or a person who arouses you sexually, to prevent the *mettā* you want to develop turning into a passionate or lustful state of mind. Although this can be very pleasant, it is not the aim of *mettā* meditation.

4. See chapter 20.

5. As a type of tranquillity meditation (see the exercise mentioned above, and the next chapter) the *brahmavihāra* play a significant role, and they are the object of the meditation. In the practice of insight meditation (see chapters 9 and 10) they are connected in a very subtle way with the accepting, compassionate and at the same time objective, character of mindfulness.

PART III

MEDITATION

Buddha image in Haw Pha Kaew, Vientiane, Laos

Part 3 of this book mainly deals with meditation, and consists of chapters 8, 9, 10 and 11.

Chapter 8 starts with a general introduction to the practice of meditation, followed by a short explanation of the method and effects of *samatha* or tranquillity meditation. Chapter 9 is an introduction to *vipassanā* or insight meditation, and chapter 10 gives some practical advice as regards the practice of insight meditation. Chapter 11 concludes this third part of the book with an explanation of the five powers which play an important part when we are practising insight meditation.

8

TRANQUILLITY MEDITATION

MEDITATION IN GENERAL

Meditation is the second prominent theme of the Eightfold Path. In Buddhism it is viewed as the most effective way to attain real peace, wisdom and the cessation of suffering. It can be seen as a mental training or development. Just as the body can be strong, healthy and flexible through sports or aerobics, so the mind can be through meditation.

In the dictionary, meditation is described as religious reflection or contemplation. This description, however, does not fully cover what in Buddhist psychology is meant by meditation. In Pali the term *bhāvanā* is generally used, which can be translated as 'cultivating or developing the mind'. So it implies a training process. Just as we cultivate or train in social skills, improving our social and communicative behaviour, in (Buddhist) meditation techniques we develop and strengthen wholesome mental powers like mindfulness and concentration.

Practising meditation is necessary if we really want to understand the Buddhist teachings. The last three guidelines of the Eightfold Path refer to the practice of meditation. These guidelines involve three different aspects that are important in meditation, namely 'right effort', 'right mindfulness' and 'right concentration'.

A certain effort or exertion is necessary when we meditate; this can be compared with the work we do in cultivating and maintaining a garden. Initially it takes effort to get the garden started;

afterwards it is a matter of regular and careful maintenance. When we neglect our vegetable plot for some time, weeds may grow or slugs might come, and there will be no vegetables to harvest. So 'right effort' means the initial effort needed to start to meditate and to sit still physically, as a voluntary discipline. On a deeper level it is more like 'maintaining the garden' – a subtle inner discipline and balanced effort (not too much, not too little) in relation to observing the object of meditation.[1]

In general, meditation can be divided into two main categories: tranquillity or relaxation meditation (*samatha-bhāvanā*) and insight or mindfulness meditation (*vipassanā-bhāvanā*). For both types of meditation it is important that our effort is balanced. Mindfulness as well as concentration is developed in both, except that the emphasis is different. This chapter is devoted specifically to the practice of *samatha* or tranquillity meditation.

THE METHOD OF TRANQUILLITY MEDITATION

In *samatha* or tranquillity meditation developing concentration is the main object. Concentration or one-pointedness of mind has the characteristic of not being distracted. Its function is to eliminate whatever distraction occurs, and it manifests as being unwavering or settled.

One basic object is used in *samatha* or tranquillity meditation, excluding all other objects or experiences. The *Visuddhimagga* describes in detail how forty different objects can be made and used:

- Ten material objects or *kasina*: objects from earth (clay), water, fire or air; objects that are blue, yellow, red or white; light; and confined spaces or apertures (for example an opening in a wall).
- Ten repulsive aspects or stages of decomposing corpses.

- Ten reflections and contemplations with regard to: the noble qualities of the Buddha, the Dhamma and the Sangha; virtue, generosity, *deva* or invisible beings in a blissful plane of consciousness; with regard to our death or the various aspects of having a body; and finally the contemplation of peace.
- Four noble mind states: lovingkindness, compassion, sympathetic joy, and equanimity.[2]
- Four immaterial states or domains: boundless space, boundless consciousness, emptiness and the domain of 'neither perception nor non-perception'.
- The repulsive nature of food.
- The four elements of water, earth, fire and air.

It is important to choose an object that suits us. Go to a quiet place, preferably a place where there is as little distraction as possible. Sit down and anchor your attention in the chosen basic object. When thoughts, emotions, sounds or other experiences distract you, you note this and then you return immediately to the original meditation object. This contracted and one-pointed awareness may soon give rise to a profound calmness and deep concentration. We no longer experience mental distractions and we become one with the object of meditation.

Everybody knows moments of being absorbed in something. This can happen while we are engaged in (top) sport, study or work, when making love, creating a work of art and so on. Mihalyi Csikszentmihalyi introduced the term *flow* in modern psychology to describe this state of mind. The American psychologist Daniel Goleman, author of the book *Emotional Intelligence* describes this phenomenon as follows: 'Flow is a healthy state of mind where you forget yourself, the opposite of worry and anxiety. Instead of being caught up in anxious thoughts, people in flow are so absorbed in what they are doing that they lose all awareness of themselves and the small daily worries (health, bills, even success) . . .

People in flow achieve their full potential. They do not question how they manage this, they do not think of success or failure. They are being driven by the pleasure in what they are doing.'

From this peak experience, the joyful concentration that is developed by means of calmness or relaxation meditation can be understood as a deeper form of flow. Because there is no physical (gross) activity in *samatha* meditation it is subtler.

FRUITS OF TRANQUILLITY MEDITATION

After practising for some time we may experience deep concentration and different levels of mental absorption may be realised. These are called *jhānas*. In the beginning these *jhānas* last only for a moment, but later on they can be experienced more easily and for longer periods, depending on the circumstances and the ability of the meditator. In that sense it can be compared to a computer game: we are able to achieve a higher level of the game more easily and more quickly.

The *Visuddhimagga* describes nine different levels of *jhāna* or concentrated absorption, which are developed step by step and become more profound. In order to avoid a technical discourse, it suffices to mention here that these nine *jhānas* involve deepening levels of concentration as we continue to practise. Thoughts disappear, and in the highest *jhānas* profound feelings of joy and happiness dissolve into a sea of tranquillity, concentration and peace.

Abiding in *jhāna* is very refreshing and calming. In normal daily life, we are often controlled by emotions we experience as problematic or as a distraction. In Buddhist psychology five of these hindrances or *nivarana* are mentioned:

1. Sensual desire (*kāmacchanda*)
2. Aversion (*byāpāda*)

3. Lethargy and sleepiness (*thina-middha*)
4. Restlessness and worry (*uddhacca-kukkucca*)
5. Doubt (*vicikicchā*)

Just as in a pond with muddy water we cannot see the bottom, likewise it seems very difficult to make wise decisions when we are ruled by or live under the influence of one or more of these emotions. In daily life these hindrances can frustrate our efforts to live in a balanced and harmonious way, and they often cause problems, especially when we cannot cope with them in a skilful manner.[3]

In the practice of *samatha* meditation the *nivarana* become less and less prominent, and they disappear when *jhāna* is achieved. The mind is clear and relaxed, temporarily free from the everyday disturbances or hindrances. The effect of developing concentration and abiding in *jhāna* can be compared to taking a cool bath on a hot day. It feels good, it is cooling and refreshing, and it quickly and pleasantly relieves tiredness and tension. In daily life this can result in us being more gentle and relaxed. Furthermore, meditators who are sensitive and sufficiently motivated seem capable of developing all kinds of supernatural powers through this form of meditation. In the classical Buddhist texts the following extraordinary powers are mentioned:

- He walks through walls or fences unhindered; he goes through mountains as if moving through air.
- He can enter into the ground and emerge from it.
- He can walk on water.
- Sitting cross-legged he can fly through the air like a bird.
- He can touch the moon and the sun.[4]
- He develops the 'divine ear' (clair-audience).
- He can penetrate the mind of others, and develops telepathic powers.

- He can remember his previous lives.
- He develops the 'divine eye' and can see invisible beings, as well as processes of cause and effect that are not visible with the ordinary human eye.

The Buddha and many of his disciples were said to have these powers. According to the scriptures, it was the Venerable Moggallāna in particular who was endowed with supernormal powers. The Buddha himself, however, was always reluctant to show these powers. He really only used them as a teaching tool to clarify a point to someone. He did not pride himself in having these supernormal gifts and clearly stated that they were not the aim of (tranquillity) meditation but a by-product. They may be useful but they also have their limitations. The following story will illustrate this.

In India at the time of the Buddha there was an ascetic who was very accomplished in *samatha* meditation. He could remain in deep *jhāna* for a long time, and he had developed the skill to levitate and fly through the air like a bird. One day he woke up in the morning with the wish to visit a fellow ascetic. He noted that the wind was exactly blowing from the right direction, and because his friend lived quite a distance away, he decided to test his psychic powers instead of walking. He concentrated on his meditation object and soon reached a deep level of *jhāna*. Then he levitated, and when he had risen above the treetops, the wind took him in the right direction.

All went well until he reached the vicinity of a castle, where he heard beautiful, soft singing. He realised he should not let himself be distracted from his meditation object, so he ignored the sound. But as the wind blew him closer and closer to the castle, the singing became clearer. The ascetic recognised it as the beautiful voice of a girl and he became curious. He did not get distracted, however, until he hovered right over the castle when the exquisite singing became so tempting that he could not prevent himself from looking down. Just at that moment the singer, a beautiful princess, came out of a tower and while she was singing started to undress to go sunbathing. The ascetic looked and looked and looked again . . . All kinds of emotions and thoughts arose in him, he forgot what he was doing, and he dropped down like a heavy stone.

I never heard how that story ended, but in any case it was not a happy ending.

This story clearly illustrates the limitations of psychic powers. They are good and beautiful, but are not everlasting in nature. They are impermanent, and difficult to deal with at times. If for instance we could read every thought in the world, but would not be able to cope with desire, aggression, fear, jealousy and other emotions, these kinds of powers would not contribute to more harmony and inner freedom. This was why the Buddha always stressed the limited merits of paranormal powers.

Samatha meditation can provide refreshing ease and calmness, however, and in that sense it is stress reducing. Tranquillity meditation is also beneficial for people who have problems with phobias, and who suffer concentration and sleep disorders. In the work I do in psychiatry, I have used relaxation exercises with young people who experience these difficulties. The relaxation exercises were based on *samatha* meditation, and it was striking how calming and relaxing these exercises were.

Clinical research has shown another beneficial effect, as described in Daniel Goleman's book, *The Meditative Mind.* Two groups of volunteers were tested in a laboratory; one group consisted of meditation facilitators, the other of people who were interested in meditation but did not have any experience in this field. The test results showed that people who were familiar with the practice of meditation could recover more quickly from stressful situations.

The spaciousness that arises from relaxation and peacefulness offers new creative possibilities. In the workplace the benefit of this is slowly being acknowledged, and businessmen are beginning to view a short practice of calmness meditation as sound investment.

Specific types of tranquillity meditation can also be extremely valuable as an antidote or remedy when somebody might find it difficult to cope with overwhelming emotions on a regular basis, and get stuck. Practising the four *brahmavihāra* can have a softening or soothing effect when we are ruled by feelings of hatred for ourselves or others, by cruelty, jealousy or too much involvement. Meditating on the different aspects of having a body may temper sensual desire and contemplation of generosity or the Dhamma reinforces a basic feeling of self-confidence and security.

Samatha meditation can be a good foundation for developing insight. I will say more about this in the next chapters.

NOTES

1. In chapter 11 I will say more about right effort.

2. See the previous chapter for these sublime mental states.

3. In chapter 13 a more detailed description will be given of the *nivarana* in the second stage of the purification process.

4. This can be taken literally, but also as a metaphor to indicate the extent of these powers.

9

INSIGHT MEDITATION

In the previous chapter I briefly described the practice and the benefits of *samatha* meditation. The Buddha knew that this type of meditation is very beneficial and that it temporarily releases us from suffering. However, he also found that practising *samatha* meditation does not ultimately provide a true remedy for life's problems. While abiding in *jhāna*, great peace and happiness are experienced. In normal, daily life however, troublesome or destructive emotions may still be there, disturbing our equilibrium and sometimes making any kind of balance or harmony impossible.

Furthermore, tranquillity meditation can also create a duality because unconsciously, through lack of insight, we may start to distinguish between the peacefulness and calmness of the meditation on the one hand, and the reality of everyday problems on the other. The deeper our sense of peacefulness and serenity in meditation, the more painful we experience our hectic life outside of meditation. And in that case the practice can result in a feeling of alienation, and cause us to turn away or flee from unresolved or unprocessed problems, which is not solving anything either. In this way meditation does not contribute to greater stability and harmony in our lives.

Buddhist psychology acknowledges seven latent obstacles or tendencies inherent in human existence which may lead to emotional and social problems. These seven tendencies or *anusayas* are:

- Sensual desire (*kāmarāga*)
- The desire to be or become somebody or something (*bhavarāga*)
- Aggression, hatred, anger (*patigha*)
- Pride, arrogance, feeling superior or inferior to others (*māna*)
- Wrong view of reality (*ditthi*)
- Doubt, uncertainty (*vicikicchā*)
- Ignorance, delusion (*avijjā*)

All our unwholesome tendencies, for instance the tendency to become jealous or to be miserly, can be fitted into one of these seven categories. These *anusaya* may be seen as strong and difficult inclinations that easily cause problems and pain, and can even ruin a person or the whole world.

In Buddhism ignorance is seen as the root cause of all these impurities. This does not imply the absence of intellectual capabilities. Rather it is not being aware or having a mistaken interpretation of what is happening in us in the present moment, which enables the seven latent tendencies to become manifest. This often causes us to deal unskilfully with emotions, thoughts, and the like. The result is that we suppress or become dependent, and that we are unaware or only half-aware of what we are doing, and consequently get into difficulties. Through ignorance we cling to pleasant thoughts and feelings, and we build up a resistance to what we experience as unpleasant. In this way an ever-increasing unwholesome burden is accumulated that we carry with us throughout our lives. Because of attachment we are afraid to lose things, we become sad when we have lost a loved one, we get jealous, angry, and so on. It is like a rolling snowball that won't stop, getting bigger and heavier and more difficult to manage all the time, and it may even become a destructive force like an avalanche.

Therapy may help to make that burden bearable and to lighten it,[1] but it cannot melt the entire snowball. Neither does belief in a higher power that protects and helps us, offer a solution for this universal, human problem. No matter how much strength we may find in such a belief, the latent tendencies will not go away, and they continue to create difficulties in our lives.

The Buddha too, in his search for enlightenment, was looking for a way to find the cause of the universal problem of suffering, and to eradicate it. Even though – according to the scriptures – he was very skilled in developing and abiding in various levels of concentration, he did not see them as a means to final liberation from the problems in life. After a long, inner search, he discovered – while he was meditating under the *bodhi* tree – a simple but at the same time very profound therapy or way of healing. This cure consists of developing mindfulness, and it leads to more acceptance of and insight into human existence; besides, this method slowly but surely results in being less conditioned by the unwholesome tendencies that so often govern our lives.

The Buddha clearly stated, particularly in the *Satipatthāna Sutta*, the teaching on the four so-called foundations of mindfulness: that true inner liberation ultimately can only be realised by means of cultivating mindfulness.[2]

A translation of this core teaching is given in appendix 1, and it is applied in the practice of *vipassanā* or insight meditation.

TWO PATHS TO INSIGHT

In fact the Buddha discovered and showed two ways in which the happiness of insight and inner freedom may be realised. In the first method initially deep states of concentration or absorption (the *jhāna*) are developed. When the meditator has become skilled in this, he or she can begin to develop mindfulness when the various factors of the *jhāna* like joy, well-being and peace of mind, dissolve again once the state of absorption is ended. In Buddhism this method is called *samatha-yānika*, insight developed on the basis of (literally, with the vehicle of) tranquillity or *samatha* meditation. The Buddha himself applied this first way of practice, and it is very suitable for people who can easily live in isolation and quiet surroundings for a long time. These are the preconditions for being able to develop the necessary concentration.

The disadvantage of this method is that Western people who are occupied with their families and jobs cannot retreat for an extended period like monks and nuns. Furthermore, making the change from developing and being absorbed in concentration to the objective observation of what is happening in the present moment proves to be much more difficult in practice than it seems on paper. Absorption of the mind is very blissful, and we can easily get attached to the *jhāna*. Because of this many meditators do not feel like switching to the cultivation of mindfulness. They (unknowingly) cling to the blissful and peaceful *jhāna*, and therefore the happiness of insight cannot be obtained.

To a certain extent this can be compared to having a job in which we are reasonably satisfied. When we're offered a different or new position, we will not immediately accept it. The new job may be more challenging and pleasant, and offer better perks. Yet – out of attachment and from fear of losing something – we are not inclined to let go of our familiar job. So this tendency can be an obstacle on the path to insight that is based on tranquillity meditation.

Later on the Buddha pointed out a second path. Here we do not need to develop strong concentration, but we cultivate mindfulness from the beginning. This method is called *suddha vipassanā-yānika*, pure or direct *vipassanā* meditation as the way or method to realise insight and inner freedom. In this second approach concentration is also developed, but in a much lighter form.[3] From the start we focus on cultivating mindfulness; we observe and register whatever occurs in body and mind from moment to moment. This second approach is actually more appropriate for (Western) people who do not have the opportunity to retreat for many weeks to accomplish the *jhāna*. Besides, this path can be more easily integrated into daily life, because all everyday mental and physical experience is used as an object of meditation. In this way meditation practice is not an (unconscious) escape, but a path to inner deepening and practical wisdom.

Vipassanā or insight meditation can be seen as a life therapy discovered by the Buddha and passed on from generation to generation. In Southeast Asia it was mainly the Venerable Mahāsi Sayadaw (who passed away in 1982) who rehabilitated this form of meditation. Through the initiative of this Burmese Buddhist monk the technique of *vipassanā* meditation has also become widely known in other parts of the world. This treasure that originated in the East is now being integrated into Western society.[4]

Insight meditation is a well-tried and unique method. It not only has a purifying and healing effect on our personality, but it also provides us with intuitive insights into the impermanent, unsatisfactory and uncontrollable or ungovernable nature of life. It is a form of meditation that everybody, irrespective of race, colour or religion, can choose. Not only does it teach us to deal more wisely with problems and blockages, but it also gives us the chance to develop more insight and stability in coping with our everyday experiences. Ultimately the highest freedom may be realised, which transcends all worldly experiences.

In the next chapter some practical guidelines will be offered with respect to this second path to inner freedom – the method of (direct) insight meditation.

NOTES

1. See chapter 17.

2. The late Venerable Nyanaponika Mahathera, a German monk with a deep knowledge of Buddhism, called these foundations of mindfulness 'the heart of Buddhist meditation' (he wrote a book of the same title).

3. See chapter 11 for more details about the various forms of concentration.

4. In the Netherlands it was a Thai monk, Venerable Mettāvihāri – my first meditation teacher – who introduced the practice of insight meditation. Many people have now become familiar with this practice, and there are various centres and sitting groups in the Netherlands where *vipassanā* meditation can be practised. In the U.K. there is Gaia House, and in the U.S. there are the Insight Meditation Society and other centres where this form of meditation is practised and taught. See appendix 4 for useful addresses.

10

THE PRACTICE OF INSIGHT MEDITATION

BASIC PRINCIPLES OF INSIGHT MEDITATION

Vipassanā or insight meditation is a technique that originates in Buddhism as it is practised in Southeast Asia.

It is a method of meditation that focuses on developing mindfulness, being able to learn to observe our own experiences directly and without bias or preference. Clear and liberating insight may arise and we begin to understand how we function as human beings, and how we can deal in a (more) skilful way with the ups and downs of life. Through the practice of insight meditation we can become aware of mental and physical phenomena in ourselves. (In our daily lives we are usually not aware or only superficially aware of these.) It is a process of coming home to what is arising in or around us in the here and now, a process of awakening with the aim of realising clarity, purity of mind and liberating insight.

It doesn't matter what philosophy of life we have. The main thing is to begin to study and observe our own lives in an open and honest way, without preconceptions or ideas. These observations are not made in an intellectual manner, but rather through paying close attention, and at the same time naming or noting whatever presents itself in or to us, from moment to moment. We do not need to analyse, reflect on or judge what we perceive.

I will give some practical guidelines for the practice of sitting, walking, prostrating and reclining meditation. Some illustrations with possible sitting and reclining postures are included, as well as some drawings to clarify the walking meditation and prostration exercises. The chapter is concluded with some advice for meditation in daily life.

EXERCISE: SITTING MEDITATION

First of all it is important to adopt a posture that is easy and relaxing so that you can sit still for a longer period of time. A cushion may help in this. You can put one under your buttocks, and perhaps one (or more) under your knees, so that you are grounded and can easily sit up straight. Loosen tight belts to give your belly room to expand. You can put your hands together in your lap, or on your thighs. The back should be straight, but not in a rigid manner. You can close your eyes.

If you have difficulty sitting cross-legged, you can also sit on a kneeling bench. And when you are older, or have specific physical difficulties, you can always sit on a chair.

Every time you become aware of (mentally) seeing or hearing, smelling, tasting, touching or thinking, or of a (pleasant or unpleasant) physical or mental feeling, you name or register this sensation or perception without going into the content of the phenomenon. Neither do you repress, avoid or escape from it. You don't need to try to change the experience. Whether you feel calm or tense, happy or sad, feel pain or sit comfortably, it really does not matter; it is fine the way you feel in this moment. There is no need to change anything.

It is particularly important to name or note as objectively as possible whatever is presenting itself, one object at a time, and always the object which at that moment is most clearly and easily perceived.

This can be anything: hearing, seeing, thinking, feeling, and so on. However, in order to be able to develop mindfulness in an easy manner, it is helpful to use one object as our basic object or starting point. In this method of meditation we use the rising and falling of the abdomen. When breathing in and out the (lower) abdomen rises and falls; these two movements are easily perceived. You will notice that the abdomen distends or rises when you breathe in, and lowers or falls when you breathe out. You can be aware of these movements.

In order to get more precision in your power of observation, and to have some objective distance from what you observe, mentally naming or noting these movements is a valuable tool. The rising of the abdomen can mentally be registered as 'rising', the falling as 'falling'. When the movements cannot be perceived clearly, you may put the palm of your left or right hand on the abdomen for a while.

In any case you don't need to change your breathing! Do not make it slower, quicker or deeper than it is of its own accord. Breathe naturally and name the rising and falling of the abdomen as these processes occur by themselves. Name mentally, not out loud.

For *vipassanā* meditation it does not matter what word you use or in what language you name. What is most important is to know or to be aware of the object. Naming or registering what is perceived is a tool that supports our observation, and it can be seen as a whisper in the background.

While you are aware of the rising and falling of the abdomen, you name or note these movements simultaneously and accordingly. Name each movement in such a way that it

is concurrent with the awareness of the movement. Awareness and naming or registering should be concurrent and synchronous, just like a stone that is thrown hits its target. Being aware of, and naming or noting the rising and falling movements of the abdomen, is one aspect of what in the *Satipatthāna Sutta* is called *kāyānupassanā*, mindfulness of the body.

After you have been sitting in meditation for some time, feelings of discomfort or stiffness may arise in your body. When these feelings become prominent, you can see them as a new object of meditation, and name them, the very moment you become clearly aware of them. You can do the same with feelings of pain, itchiness, tiredness, heaviness or lightness in the body, ease or relaxation, heat or cold. Here too, you don't need to try to get rid of the feeling or to 'observe to make them go away'. Neither do you give them extra attention. You only need to be aware of the feeling and name or note as it is recognised. You can do this for as long as the feeling presents itself and as long as it is perceived clearly. When the feeling retreats to the background, or dissolves by itself, then you can be aware again of the rising and falling movement of the abdomen and name or register these processes. If the feeling remains, you continue to register it as long as it manifests itself clearly. However, when the feeling becomes unbearable you do not need to force yourself to keep

still. You can slowly and quietly change your posture, meanwhile observing and naming what is happening. Dealing with physical sensations in this manner is an aspect of what in Pali is called *vedanānupassanā*, mindfulness of feelings.

Perhaps your mind wanders while you are observing and naming the movements of the belly. Whenever you become aware of this, you should observe this as well. Sometimes a thought stops as soon as it is recognised. Then you don't need to do anything with it, because it has disappeared already. You can register the next object that presents itself. However, when the thought is still there at the moment of recognition, you can note or register its presence. When the thought presents itself as wandering, you name it as 'wandering', 'wandering', 'wandering'. When you have named it once, twice or three times and the mind has stopped wandering of its own accord, you return to the awareness and recognition of the rising and falling of the abdomen. When you are remembering something, you name it as 'reflecting', 'reflecting', 'reflecting,' or as 'remembering', 'remembering', 'remembering', 'remembering'. If in your mind you meet someone, you can name this as 'meeting', 'meeting'. When you are having a mental conversation with somebody, you name this as 'talking', 'talking', and so on.

In short, whatever thought or reflection may arise, the moment you recognise it you

can see it as a meditation object, and name or register it, as it is recognised and as long it is prominent. Do not spend too much time trying to find the right word for a thought. Recognising it is more important, and the first word or label that comes to mind will do. So when you recognise a thought as a fantasy, you note it as 'imagining'; when you are thinking, as 'thinking'; when you are making plans, as 'planning'; when you are judging something, as 'judging'; when you are worrying, as 'worrying'; and so on.

Usually you name or register the thought a few times and then you are aware again of the rising and falling of the abdomen (or of something else that may be predominant in that moment). But if the thought is persistent and does not disappear, you should continue to name it, as long as it is clearly present and keeps demanding your attention.

Very often we are not aware, or do not succeed in registering these mental activities, so we have the tendency to identify ourselves with them. We tend to think that there is an 'I' who is imagining, thinking, judging, making plans, knowing or perceiving. We think there is a person who has lived and thought since birth, whereas in reality there are only these continuing and successive mental activities. The more we identify with experiences – our position in life, with things and people – the heavier our problems or the baggage we carry around with us become. When all these experiences disappear, dissolve or get lost, we begin to miss them, feel fear or anger because of our attachment to and identification with them. Therefore it is advisable to name or note each and every cognitive activity the moment it is clearly recognised. It is a remedy for the universal human tendency of attachment and identification, or – when a thought is experienced as unpleasant – the problem of aversion and conflict.

It is important to point out that it is not necessary to get involved with the content of the thought. You don't need to find out why you are thinking, or where, when or with whom a memory took place. On the other hand you also do not need to get rid of a thought or name it 'in order for it to go away'. It is sufficient just to observe and register the thought as a phenomenon, without getting involved or trying to stop it. When the thought has disappeared of its own accord, or has dissolved, you can return to the awareness and naming of the rising and falling of the abdomen. Observing and registering all these mental activities is an aspect of *cittānupassanā*, mindfulness of thinking and of the mind.

While observing and naming or registering the rising and falling of the abdomen, there is no need to look for other experiences or objects. But it may happen that you become aware of a sound, and that this takes your attention away from the abdomen. At that moment you don't need to consider it a distraction, but you can see it as a new meditation object, and observe and register it as 'hearing', 'hearing', 'hearing', as long as the sound is clearly recognisable. Or you may see images with closed eyes; then you can name this (mental) seeing, as long as it is clearly there.

You don't need to consider the sound or the image as a distraction. See it as a new meditation object, just as valuable as rising, falling, physical feelings or thoughts. Again, there is no need to concern yourself with the content of what you see or hear, nor do you need to try to get rid of the sound or the image. However, sometimes you recognise a sound or an image, and you interpret it as 'train', 'car', 'neighbour' or 'tree'. In those moments you can name as 'interpreting', or as 'recognising'; otherwise you just observe the seeing, hearing, smelling or touching.

Apart from these sensory experiences there are all kinds of other experiences you might have during the meditation practice, like moments of impatience, or irritation in relation to pain, thoughts or sitting still. Or there may be moments of enjoyment, desire, doubt, uncertainty, sleepiness, worry or restlessness. When a reaction or emotion like this arises in you, again you don't need to judge it as a distraction or a disturbance. The emotional reaction can be integrated into the meditation process by simply recognising and naming it as 'impatience', 'impatience', 'enjoying', 'enjoying', 'uncertain', 'uncertain', and so on, the moment it presents itself clearly. It is good to realise that these experiences are just as valuable as a meditation object as the rising and falling of the belly, hearing a sound, a physical sensation or a thought.

Perhaps other emotional feelings become predominant, such as feelings of happiness, joy, rapture, tranquillity, sadness, frustration, disappointment, remorse, boredom, confidence or enthusiasm. You only need to observe these emotions and name or note them – as they are and as long as they are clearly recognisable – as 'happy', 'happy', 'sad', 'sad', or 'calm', 'calm', according to the nature of the emotions. There is no need to do anything else. Naming or noting this last and fourth category is called *dhammānupassanā*, mindfulness of mental and physical phenomena in general, with particular reference to the phenomena we experience in our meditation practice that are not mentioned in the first three categories.

In short, it can be said that we are always observing and naming or noting what is happening in body and mind. Without preference or aversion, like or dislike, we observe and register whatever is clearly recognisable and predominant in the present moment. Essentially it does not matter what kind of object it is. Whether it is a thought, a physical sensation, a sound, a pleasant or unpleasant emotion, or the rising and falling of the abdomen, all these experiences are of equal value. They can be seen as a meditation object the moment they clearly show themselves; one at a time, and always that which is predominant in a given moment. In this sense mindfulness is a flexible quality of mind, which from moment to moment can have a different experience as its object.

However, do not try to do too much. For instance, it is not necessary to try hanging on to or getting rid of experiences. Neither do you need to force yourself, trying to name or note something that has already disappeared or is not clearly recognisable.

Keep it simple. It is sufficient to limit yourself to what is clearly present or recognisable in this moment. You don't even need to look for objects, they will present themselves in their own time. You sit up straight in a relaxed way, and you simply observe and register whatever is prominent and perceivable in the moment, without interfering in the process.

There is no need to make anything clearer, to try and hold on to it, make it disappear or to suppress it. Just merely observe and register a mental or physical experience as it presents itself, and as long as it is predominant. Don't let the naming or registering become a heavy burden either. As you continue to practise, you will become more familiar with it and it will become more fluid. Ultimately the most important thing is to be in touch with or aware of whatever is happening here and now; naming or noting it can be seen as a valuable and supporting tool, to strengthen the mindfulness.

When the object of observation disappears or dissolves by itself, and when at that moment nothing else is clearly recognisable, in this meditation technique you can always return to the awareness and naming or noting of the rising and falling of the abdomen as your basic object.

EXERCISE: WALKING MEDITATION

Many people think that meditation only means sitting meditation. In fact this is not true, because insight meditation can also be practised standing, reclining, walking, and in all daily activities. One method that is often used to cultivate mindfulness is the practice of walking meditation.

Find a space of three to ten metres in length to walk up and down. Stand on one side and first of all be aware of the standing posture for a while. Make sure you are grounded, the feet slightly

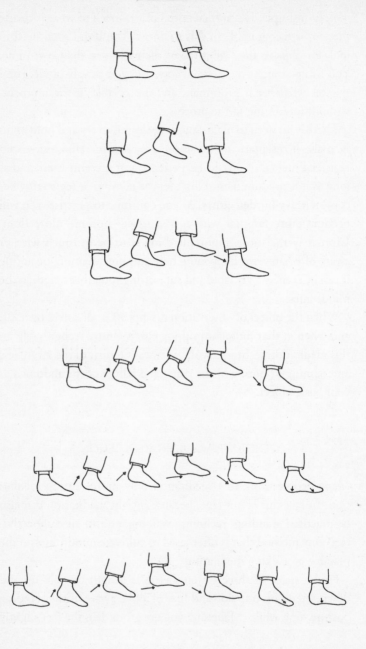

apart and the knees not locked. Keep your body relaxed and upright, arms by the sides or hands clasped in front or behind, and keep your head upright. The eyes are open, and the gaze is down two to four metres in front of you on the floor, without being focused on anything in particular. No need to look at your feet, nor straight ahead or around. This will help to create a good environment for developing (greater) continuity of mindfulness. For a short time you are aware of the standing posture of the body, naming or registering this mentally as 'standing', 'standing', 'standing'. You know that the body is in the standing posture.

Then you can note the intention to walk as 'intending', 'intending', 'intending', and start the walking meditation. It is advised to walk slowly, taking small steps, so that you can observe accurately and precisely what is happening. When you are taking a step, you observe the full movement of the foot.

You are aware of how the foot leaves the floor, moves through the air, and is put down again. The slower the step, the more precision you can have in observing the process. However, do not slow down to the extent that you keep losing your balance or fall down. To make it easier to keep your balance it is better to take small steps.

No great effort is necessary, and you don't need to force yourself or focus too much on the movements you observe. It is sufficient to be aware of the movement of the foot in a light but at the same time precise manner. While you are observing this movement, you name or note simultaneously as 'left goes thus', 'right goes thus' and so on. You can see this awareness of the movement of the foot as the basic object during the walking meditation, like the function of rising and falling of the abdomen during sitting meditation. During the walking you don't need to pay attention to the breath or the rising and falling of the abdomen.

When you have reached the end of your walking track, you put your feet together again. You are aware of the standing position for a few moments, naming as 'standing', 'standing', 'standing'.

Then you note the intention to turn as 'intending', 'intending', 'intending'. With your left or right foot you turn about sixty degrees, and you register as 'turning'. Then you put your other foot next to it, naming or noting it as 'closing'. In this way you turn sixty degrees three times, and you close the movement with the other foot. After registering standing and the intention to walk, you continue with the walking meditation.

When other objects or experiences are present in a light manner (i.e. in the background), you don't need to give them specific attention, but you just continue to walk. When something else becomes predominant – something you see with cast down eyes, or a sound, a thought, a physical sensation, smell or emotion – don't regard this as a disturbance but simply see it as a new meditation object. If it does not immediately dissolve or disappear of its own accord when you recognise it, the advice is to stop and give it attention, registering as 'hearing', 'hearing', 'seeing', 'seeing', 'thinking', 'thinking'.

It is not an enemy but a new meditation object, just as valuable as being aware of and registering the movement of the foot. For that moment you stop and note the new object, as it appears to you and as long as it is predominant. When it disappears or dissolves by itself, or is no longer predominant, you can continue the walking meditation.

You can practise walking meditation for a period of between ten and sixty minutes, depending on the time you determined beforehand. If you wish, after some time you can divide the step in different stages, thereby developing more precision in your mindfulness. In the second walking exercise you can divide the step into lifting and placing of the foot, and observe and register these two phases separately as 'lifting', 'placing', 'lifting', 'placing'. In the third walking exercise you are aware of three stages in the step, and you register as 'lifting', 'going', 'placing', 'lifting' 'going', 'placing'.

There are six different walking exercises in all, observing in more and more detail what is happening. You should not force this, however, but develop these exercises gently. It can be compared to driving a car, or learning how to drive. A car has four or five gears. When you begin to drive it would not be sensible to put the car in fourth gear straightaway. It would be too difficult for the engine, use extra fuel, and it might damage the engine as well. Besides it might be quite dangerous to start driving very fast if you have little or no driving experience. So it would be wiser not to force yourself. Therefore it is advisable in general not to do more than the first three walking exercises initially, and to build these up slowly, starting with the first exercise, doing this for some time, then doing the second and then possibly the third. Ultimately it is not about how many walking exercises you practise. The main point is that you can be aware of what is happening in body and mind in an easy, relaxed manner.

EXERCISE: PROSTRATION MEDITATION[1]

Generally speaking mostly walking and sitting meditation are used as exercises to cultivate mindfulness. But in addition and as an extra stimulus you can also practise prostration meditation. It turns out that many meditators experience stiffness in their bodies, especially when they meditate regularly. And many people find inspiration in doing the prostrations. The exercise can be practised in various ways.

Option 1.
Kneel on the floor and sit on your heels, having the toes bent. (This position of your feet has the added physical advantage of stimulating or activating a number of pressure points.) When this position is impossible because of old age or strong pain, you can

also put your feet flat on the floor. Your back is straight. Put your hands together, palms facing, and have your thumbs touch your chest at the level of your heart. This posture can be named as 'purity'. Do not visualise anything. Simply bring your attention to your heart centre, without further reflection on purity.

Slowly raise your hands until the thumbs are touching your forehead. Name this posture as 'compassion'.

With the next movement you bring your lower arms and the hands to the floor, elbows touching the knees, and palms flat on the floor. Place your forehead between your hands, relax your belly and name this position as 'wisdom'.

Then revert to the initial posture and repeat the prostration exercise a few times.

Option 2.

If you think the previous exercise is too 'religious', you can also practise it in the following way: Slowly make the same movements, and take up the same postures. Instead of naming as 'purity', 'compassion' and 'wisdom', you observe all movements and the three postures. You start in the beginning posture, and are aware of it for a while. You can register this posture as 'sitting', as 'posture' or as 'knowing' (knowing you are in this posture).

Next you register the intention to move, and you can slowly raise your arms and hands. You name or note as 'moving', 'moving', 'moving', or as 'raising', 'raising', 'raising'.

You register the thumbs touching the forehead as 'touching'. Then you are aware again of the posture, and you register this. Next you slowly bend your upper body to the floor and you name this as 'bending', 'bending', 'bending'. The contact of the hands, elbows and forehead successively with the floor is named as 'touching'. You register relaxing the belly, and the physical awareness in this posture. Finally you slowly raise your upper body again, and you name this as 'up', 'up', 'up'. The palms of the hands touching, and the thumbs against your chest, is registered again as 'touching', and you are returning to the initial position. When other experiences are predominant while practising this exercise, you can be aware of these and then resume the prostration exercise, as we do in the walking meditation.

Option 3.
You can also combine the previous two exercises by observing and registering the movements and the experience of contact. The three postures can be named as 'purity', 'compassion' and 'wisdom'.

If you wish you can do this exercise before every sitting or walking meditation. It has a beneficial effect and often works as a healthy form of 'auto-physiotherapy'. The exercise may also inspire us. And it can be used to create some distance from our daily cares and worries, enabling us to focus more on the here and now.

Some people feel quite a bit of resistance when reading or hearing about the prostration exercise. You might think it is too religious. In that case you can name the resistance as a meditation object, but do not force yourself. If you can't see any benefit, just skip this exercise, realising it is not a must, but merely an additional exercise to the walking and the sitting meditation.

EXERCISE: RECLINING MEDITATION

Vipassanā meditation can also be practised lying down. To do this, lie down on your back comfortably. You may need to put a pillow under your head. Put your arms alongside your body and your hands (touching) on top of your belly. You can also lie down on your right side[2], and when you have any physical difficulties, there are variations possible that allow you to lie still for some time. For the rest, the same guidelines apply as for the sitting meditation.

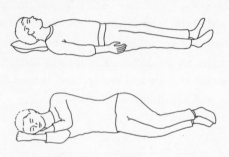

MEDITATION IN DAILY LIFE

Something needs to be clarified about the time you might spend practising meditation. In fact there are no strict rules, and any period between five and sixty minutes is fine.

Nevertheless, many teachers advise to choose a period of about thirty minutes, in order to 'get into it' and to gain some depth. But it depends on the time and space you have at your disposal, and on your motivation. So when thirty minutes seems too long, twenty-five minutes is fine too. And when twenty-five minutes is too long, then twenty will do, and so on. Some teachers stress a regular, preferably daily, practice, like a daily wash, out of care and respect for ourselves and others. Other meditation instructors are more pragmatic: practise when you wish and are able.

With a little bit of creativity we can also transform so-called 'dead moments' or 'trivial activities' into moments of meditation. Sitting in a train or a bus or in a doctor's waiting room can – with the support of the guidelines for the sitting meditation – become a source of insight, inner peace and stability.

Sitting, walking, prostrating and reclining meditation can be seen as basic exercises. Essentially you can cultivate mindfulness during the most mundane everyday activities. As an explicit exercise you can – if you have the time and space – slow down your movements during an activity somewhat, and observe carefully what is happening physically and mentally. The following is an example of this.

EXERCISE: MINDFULLY EATING A BISCUIT

First of all you can become aware that you are sitting, and of the rising and falling of the belly. Register seeing the biscuit and the desire to pick it up. Observing and noting the movements slowly extend your arm in the direction of the biscuit. Then you name picking it up. Move your other hand in the direction of the biscuit, and register breaking off a small piece.

As you become aware of the lifting movement of your arm you register this; you also name or note opening your mouth and putting the piece of biscuit in your mouth.

You can also register the contact between the piece of biscuit and the inside of the mouth. Name the intention to chew, and observe and register chewing.

Perhaps the taste or the liking of the biscuit becomes predominant; in that case you register this. Next you can be aware of swallowing and feeling the chewed substance going down through the oesophagus to the stomach.

Finally you eat the rest of the biscuit, observing and registering as you do so.

This is a simple example of cultivating mindfulness in daily activities. Washing up, brushing our teeth, shaving or going to the toilet can become mindfulness practices.

However, sitting, walking and prostrating prove to be the most suitable basic postures for developing mindfulness. When practising reclining meditation it is much easier to lose clarity of mind, because in that position it is not necessary to exert ourselves to keep physically upright or to move. Hence our attention slackens easily during reclining. And in our daily activities we easily become careless, prematurely ending the meditation exercise due to everyday hurry, worry and other conditionings.

Regularity and patient discipline in the practice reinforce mindfulness and inner stability in general. But be realistic instead of idealistic when determining how much time you want to spend on (daily) meditation practice. If it turns out to be impossible to free up some time for practice every day, do not feel guilty. Nothing is compulsory, it is a natural path, without force or constraint. You can also just meditate when you feel the need and have the time.

But when you want to meditate, it is always advisable to choose a time and a space with as few disturbances as possible. A few hints:

- Unplug the telephone or switch on the answering machine.
- Create a space in your home specifically for meditation.
- Pick a time when you are alone.
- When partner or children are present you might indicate beforehand that you want to practise meditation for a certain period, and that you do not wish to be disturbed unnecessarily.
- Put an egg timer or alarm clock somewhere, which you have set to go off after a certain predetermined time.

In conclusion I would like to say something about guidance in learning how to meditate. If you are really interested in *vipassanā* meditation and want to explore it more, it is advisable to get in touch with one of the centres or contacts mentioned in appendix 3. It is very important to have some guidance if you want to become familiar with the meditation method and go deeper. Having a teacher does not mean that you become dependent, but that you to learn to walk the subtle spiritual path, so that after some time you begin to understand your own meditative process. In order to fill this need, there are weekly sitting groups, weekend and longer retreats where people meditate together, and where guidance is given. Anybody who wants to learn to walk the spiritual path is welcome, and experienced meditators often feel these gatherings are an additional source of inspiration.

NOTES

1. Buddhists often prostrate three times as a form of respect. During the first prostration they pay respect to the Buddha, during the second to the Dhamma, and during the third to the Sangha (the community of Dhamma practitioners).

2. By lying on your right side there will be no pressure on the heart area.

II

FIVE POWERS

Buddhist psychology often refers to five beneficial powers, which can be developed through the practice of *vipassanā* meditation. In Pali these powers are called *indriya*, mental qualities or faculties that play an important part in the meditation process, and that begin to have a healing effect on how we live our day-to-day lives. The five *indriya* are (self-) confidence, effort, mindfulness, concentration and wisdom.

1. CONFIDENCE (*SADDHĀ*)

First of all this relates to confidence we have in the meditation practice and in our own abilities. Gradually confidence in the Buddha, his teachings (the Dhamma) and/or the people who practise and have realised his teachings (the Sangha) will grow as well.

In the Commentaries[1] the five powers are described according to characteristic, function and manifestation. The presence of faith or (self-)confidence is mentioned as the characteristic of *saddhā*. Confidence or trust has a purifying function, and is manifested as clarity and certainty. It empowers us to act resolutely and with confidence. Faith or confidence is mentioned as the first *indriya* because it is the force that motivates us to follow a spiritual path.

2. EFFORT (*VIRIYA*)

The term *viriya* can imply many meanings, such as effort, energy, diligence or courage. The characteristics of effort are patience and perseverance; it is the courageous effort not to give up when we encounter difficulties and temptations on the path of meditation. Its function is to support and strengthen mindfulness. Effort is manifested as a strong and courageous determination not to give up or break off our undertakings halfway or before they are finished. It arises from a sense of urgency as the result of seeing the instability or insecurity of existence.

The fire of *viriya* becomes very clear in the vow the ascetic Gotama made when he sat down under the *bodhi* tree and determined not to get up until he had realised the highest wisdom. *Even though my flesh and blood may dry up, and only skin, bones and sinews may be left; even though I may die, I shall not give up.*

This is a very determined declaration, and perhaps we do not need to go that far in our intentions. Nevertheless, effort is a very important factor in dealing with emotional and physical pain in our meditation practice. We do not shift our posture, or run away from the problem, but we continue to observe it in an accepting and patient manner, in order to learn from the pain. In this way the difficulties we encounter in our meditation practice become friends instead of enemies. In dealing with pleasant mental or physical feelings, too, effort is important, so that we are not blinded by these feelings, which would hinder the progress of insight. It is an art not to get attached to a pleasant feeling when we are practising, but to view this too as a meditation object, and not as a goal in itself.

In everything we do effort is an important factor; not to give up and to finish what we started.

3. MINDFULNESS, ATTENTIVENESS (*SATI*)

In English *sati* is mostly translated as 'mindfulness' or 'recollection', meaning a careful yet unforced observation. In his book *Thoughts without a Thinker,* Mark Epstein describes it as 'remembering the present'. The power of observation, which is called mindfulness throughout this book, has two aspects. On the one hand there is an open and accepting awareness of the mental or physical experience of what is in or around us in the moment. On the other hand there is a subtle and objective noting, cognitively recognising or registering the experience that is perceived in that moment.

The characteristic of *sati* is presence of mind. Its function is not to forget, not to neglect or skip over what is predominant in the here and now. Mindfulness manifests as protection against unknowingly being (more) conditioned by thoughts, emotions and sensory input, and against unwholesome mental states. Mindfulness is supported by a balanced effort.

In the *Satipatthāna Sutta,* four foundations for developing mindfulness are mentioned:

1. The body. Examples of this first foundation are the rising and falling of the abdomen, the posture of the body or the (walking) movements of the body.
2. Feelings. This includes physical pain, itchiness, heat, cold, tension or stiffness. Apart from such unpleasant physical sensations, it also means pleasant physical sensations. Mental (pleasant, unpleasant and neutral) feelings are included in this category as well.
3. Thoughts. Examples are contemplations, memories, fantasies or reflections. Judging, analysing, planning thoughts or other cognitive processes are also part of the third foundation of mindfulness.

4. Phenomena in general. This includes emotions or mental states like anger, fear, restlessness, doubt, attachment and desire. All other phenomena that may arise (like sensory perceptions) and those that have not been mentioned in the first three categories, are included in this last foundation.[2]

The four foundations of mindfulness may be compared to four meadows that can be used by a cow to graze and to yield high quality milk. They may also be viewed as the necessary foundations for building a house (of insight). If one or more of the foundations is not built properly or is not strong enough, the house may collapse. This analogy indicates that all four foundations of mindfulness are of equal importance as a precondition for the cultivation of insight.

Mindfulness is the most important of the five powers. Without mindfulness it is impossible to bring the four other *indriya* into equilibrium and to keep them balanced. My Burmese teacher, Achan Asabha, abbot of the *vipassanā* meditation centre Wat Vivek Asom in Chonburi, Thailand, compared the function of mindfulness with that of a Prime Minister who is the pivot in a team of five ministers. The other four ministers each have a specific task, but ultimately the Prime Minister co-ordinates them.

4. CONCENTRATION (*SAMĀDHI*)

This minister has the characteristic of not being absent-minded and distracted. The function of concentration is to gather or bundle consciousness into one object; its manifestation is one of calm one-pointedness of mind.

Samādhi could be described as the focus or the magnifying glass through which the object of meditation is being observed. Three types can be distinguished:

1. Access or 'approaching' concentration (*upacāra-samādhi*)
2. Absorption or full concentration (*appanā-samādhi*)
3. Momentary concentration (*khaṇika-samādhi*)

The first two forms of concentration are mostly developed through *samatha* meditation, where the emphasis is on realising deep and blissful types of absorption or *jhāna*. Such a level of concentration can be achieved by focusing the mind on one specific object, excluding all other objects.[3] In the beginning this will result in 'approaching' concentration, and when the *jhāna* are realised there is full concentration or *appanāa-samādhi*.[4]

The third form of concentration is mainly developed during the practice of *vipassanā* meditation. In this practice the emphasis is on what is happening in the present moment, without getting absorbed into one specific object. So in *vipassanā* meditation there are many more objects, because every physical or mental experience is suitable as a meditation object. A light momentary concentration is enough. And we always maintain a subtle distance from the object, by naming or noting it. This last type of concentration is cultivated drop by drop, and slowly but surely it will deepen, without becoming dominant or controlling. Mindfulness remains the strongest factor; flexible momentary concentration creates a sharper focus and gives rise to the next and last power.

5. WISDOM OR INSIGHT (*PAÑÑĀ*)

According to the Commentaries, wisdom has the characteristic of penetrating the reality of things. Its function is to shine light into the darkness. It manifests as the absence of delusion, and is produced by concentrated mindfulness.

Insight means intuitively having right or correct understanding of what is happening here and now, and of the object of observation. It refers to seeing or beginning to see certain characteristics inherent in life, namely the impermanent, unsatisfactory and un-controllable nature of existence. This realisation or insight is not based on thought, but on direct, clear seeing. Therefore the insight from *vipassanā* meditation is called intuitive. It relates to an inner knowing of how we can deal in a wise and skilful way with the vicissitudes of life. Because wisdom is a specific fruit of the practice of *vipassanā* meditation, I will say more about it in the next chapter.

The order in which the five powers are usually listed (as I did), has its reasons. Without basic confidence, trust or faith in the practice of meditation, in the teachings of the Buddha or in a meditation teacher we meet, we would not begin to practise. Even if the trust or confidence we have initially might not yet be very mature or based on insight, it is very important as an impetus to start walking the spiritual path. Because of this faith we arouse the effort to actually begin to practise; we make the effort to develop mindfulness from moment to moment.

As a direct result of a moment of mindfulness, there is at the same time a moment of concentrated or focused awareness of the object of observation (*khanika-samādhi*). This leads to intuitive insight as regards this object; we realise its impermanent, unsatisfactory and ungovernable nature.

This clear seeing of things as they really are – this insight – is the basis for a growing trust in the path of meditation, a confidence that is grounded in our own experience. This in turn results in more effort or exertion, sharper mindfulness, deeper concentration and so on.

In this way the five *indriya* are developed more and more, like an upward spiral. They become potential forces (*bala*) that purify our character. Old conditionings and impurities are recognised. By observing and registering them, without judgement or condemnation, they no longer rule us. Gradually they begin to lose their power and they will disappear. Pure consciousness arises, which is a mind more and more free from desire, hatred, ignorance and other unwholesome forces. More mindfulness is cultivated at the same time. When the five healing powers have been developed fully, and when there is great clarity of mind and a good inner balance, this insight may eventually culminate in the experience of enlightenment or *nibbāna*. At that time liberating insight is completely and perfectly realised.

We are not supposed to constantly wonder in our meditation practice exactly which healing power is being developed in those moments. When we are taking a vitamin pill, we do not wonder either which vitamin or mineral is active at any given moment. Similarly in meditation practice, we know how the five powers are being developed because we heard or read about them, but we can hardly distinguish them, especially in the beginning. So it is sufficient just to observe and name or note whatever arises in or around us from moment to moment. The results are good mental health and other fruits of the practice. I will describe these in the next chapter.

NOTES

1. The *Visuddhimagga* and the *Sammohavinodani*.

2. For more details about these four foundations of mindfulness, see chapters 9 and 10, and appendix 1.

3. See chapter 8.

4. *Appanā-samādhi* is also realised at the moment of enlightenment.

PART IV

FRUITS AND OBSTACLES

Subduing Mara', Kyaik Pun Paya, Bago, Myanmar

Part 4 of this book consists of chapters 12, 13, 14 and 15. It deals with the two most obvious fruits of the intensive practice of *vipassanā* meditation, namely intuitive wisdom or insight, and purity or clarity of mind. In chapter 12 various forms of wisdom will be discussed; chapter 13 deals with the seven stages in the process of purification. In chapter 14 I will give particular attention to the seventh stage of the purification process, namely the experience of enlightenment. In chapter 15 a number of obstacles that we can meet on the path of meditation will be discussed.

12

INTUITIVE WISDOM

In the previous chapter I described briefly what is meant in Buddhism by wisdom or insight. Wisdom or *paññā* investigates and penetrates the truth of things. It brings light in darkness, creates clarity, and is the opposite of misunderstanding, delusion or ignorance (*avijjā*).

Wisdom or insight is not just the intellectual capacity to consider things in relation to other things; it is much more like an intuitive process that does not use 'step by step' reasoning. It is the fruit of concentrated mindfulness and does not come about through the medium of thought.

In the Pali literature various synonyms are given for wisdom. The most prevalent ones are *vipassanā* (insight), *dhamma vicaya* (intuitive investigation of phenomena), *ñāna* (level of insight), and *sammā ditthi* (right or clear understanding). As 'right understanding' wisdom is the first aspect of the Eightfold Path. In chapter 3 only one facet of right understanding or right view has been touched on. However, in Buddhist psychology many more types of right or clear understanding are mentioned, which can be achieved or realised through the practice of insight meditation. I will discuss some of these forms of wisdom or insight below.

1. INSIGHT INTO THE FACT THAT WE ARE THE OWNERS OF OUR KARMA

This insight, which has already been mentioned in chapter 3, refers to the deep-rooted sense that we ourselves are responsible for all our actions, and that we will experience the results of these.

This fundamental understanding, called *kammassakatā sammā ditthi* in Pali, asks of us to cultivate discernment between what is wholesome and what is not, so that we choose a path that leads to more happiness, insight and harmony. This basic insight lies at the root of walking a spiritual path, and it is the foundation of meditation practice.

2. CLEAR AWARENESS OF MENTAL AND PHYSICAL PROCESSES

Insight meditation could be called a process of awakening: first of all we become aware of experiences we were not aware of before. This form of insight starts with the growing understanding of how little we really know about ourselves. A large part of our mental and physical experience seems to be happening unconsciously. And unconsciously we are being controlled by it.

With the practice of insight meditation gradually more mental and physical processes – of which we were previously unaware – are being 'charted'. Each moment of awareness with regard to what is clearly happening in or to us in the here and now, is also a moment of inner spaciousness. Whereas before we were unconsciously caught up in thoughts, emotions and other experiences, now there is a liberating recognition of what is going on. The journey of discovery and the liberation that is flowing from it, can be compared to the relief we may experience when we suddenly see a flicker of light after we have been lost in a dark cave.

94

3. CLEAR COMPREHENSION OF THE PROCESSES OF CAUSE AND EFFECT IN MENTAL AND PHYSICAL PHENOMENA

As a direct result of this journey of discovery, there is the unfolding of clear comprehension in relation to the processes of cause and effect that are involved in the physical and mental phenomena we have become aware of. This comprehension or understanding is not a rational analysis of why we experience certain thoughts, emotions or feelings. We are not looking for the how and why of our experience, but with the help of mindfulness, karmic connections will spontaneously begin to show themselves. This can be very clarifying and revealing, and has therapeutic effects.[1]

This third type of insight not only has healing aspects but also empirical scientific elements. We are observing the processes of cause and effect in ourselves, in an accurate and objective manner, just like a scientist is striving for an accurate and objective study of, for instance, biological phenomena. Without judging or condemning we perceive how experiences in body and mind are interrelated and interdependent. Without interference or taboos, we observe and register in detail what is appearing before us moment by moment, without (intentional) intervention of conceptual thought. The insight arising from the cultivation of mindfulness is intuitive.

Usually the second and third forms of right understanding arise together quite naturally. They could be called psychosomatic insights: the relationships between physical and mental phenomena are revealed. If the meditation process is continued, the next aspect of wisdom can be developed.

4. EXISTENTIAL WISDOM

At this level three natural laws or universal characteristics of existence are clearly revealed, namely impermanence, unsatisfactoriness and uncontrollability.

1. Impermanence: all mental and physical phenomena that are perceived turn out to be impermanent. In the texts this is stated as follows: First not existing they appear, they are present (they exist), and finally they disappear or fall away again. As a meditator we become very much aware that everything is finite.
2. Unsatisfactoriness: all worldly phenomena are a constant mental and physical burden, and therefore cannot be considered satisfactory. Some experiences or situations like war, hunger, mental or physical pain, are clearly not satisfying. However, pleasant and neutral situations, and mental or physical phenomena, are also viewed as unsatisfactory, due to their impermanent nature. The word 'unsatisfactory' says it all: we cannot find real satisfaction in them.
3. Uncontrollability: our inability to control or manipulate impermanent and unsatisfactory processes can be seen as the uncontrollable or ungovernable characteristic of existence.

This last natural law also refers to an aspect of egolessness or 'no self'. In Buddhist psychology it is said that there is no ego, no 'self' or solid and independent entity that controls our lives. Life consists of countless mental and physical experiences that are connected to each other in a process of cause and effect; this can be compared to a river, which in reality consists of nothing but millions and millions of water drops. The concept of a 'self' or an 'ego' arises through identification with what are ultimately impermanent and unsatisfactory processes; we interpret these as being 'mine' or 'me'. Based on this illusion we try to control and manipulate the river of life (often in a very forced manner). Even though we might be able to steer the course of life into a certain direction, ultimately these physical and mental processes are impermanent and ungovernable.

This fourth insight too, arises from concentrated mindfulness and is intuitive in nature. It is not connected with thought, but based on a direct, clear awareness of what is occurring here and now in body and mind.

In the next chapter I will discuss these three universal characteristics or *tilakkhana* in more detail. Clear comprehension of these three natural laws, which might be called existential insight, has various wholesome effects. A deeper understanding of impermanence results in a more flexible attitude in coping with the vicissitudes of life. There will be less fear of losing, and even of dying. The understanding of unsatisfactoriness becomes a fertile ground for greater tolerance, and for compassion with our own suffering and that of others. Fully realising that things are uncontrollable works as a cure for our tendency to try to manipulate situations in life that are outside our influence.

In short, this form of insight leads to deeper happiness and well-being. The first four insights remain in the mundane sphere, however.

5. TRANSCENDENTAL INSIGHT

The fifth insight can be realised on the basis of the previous forms of insight. In this insight ordinary worldly experience is transcended. In chapter 3 (when discussing the third noble truth) I have already mentioned the experience of *nibbāna* or enlightenment. In the *Abhidhamma* this is described as a transcendental experience consisting of two very subtle supramundane forms of conscious that very quickly follow one another: *magga* and *phala citta* or 'path-consciousness' and 'fruition-consciousness'. Both moments of consciousness have *nibbāna* as their object.

According to the scriptures the Four Noble Truths are being fully penetrated at the moment of *magga* or 'path-consciousness'. Suffering is fully understood, the cause of suffering is removed, the ending of suffering is realised, and the Eightfold Path that leads to the cessation of suffering, is fully cultivated.

Path-consciousness is described as extinguishing the fires caused by forms of desire, hatred and ignorance. *Phala* or 'fruition-consciousness' is likened to the cooling down of the heat and steam that had remained after the fire. These two types of consciousness are very subtle in nature, and according to Buddhist psychology, they succeed one another with the speed of lightning. The ordinary mental and physical processes totally disappear for a moment; at that moment there is complete and unconditioned harmony and peace.[2]

After this experience the meditator returns to mundane consciousness. This has been described as being similar to waking up from a dream and then reviewing the dream. The liberating experience of a moment ago is noted and confirmed afterwards.[3] The understanding may also arise that certain impurities in the mind have indeed been fully extinguished, or that other impurities are still present, so that there is still plenty of meditative work to be done.

WISDOM AND THE EIGHTFOLD PATH

The Eightfold Path is the practical way to these forms of intuitive wisdom, and it can be most fully realised by developing mindfulness and practising insight meditation.

Based on the first type of insight we begin to walk the spiritual path, and we start to cultivate mindfulness. The second link in the Eightfold Path – right thought – is manifested as getting in touch with or mentally hitting and becoming aware of the physical or mental experience that is predominant in the moment. In naming or noting this perception right speech is realised, for in that moment we don't tell lies, we don't gossip or curse. Neither do we talk nonsense, because we name things as they are. This is about as truthful as can be. Right action and right livelihood are observed by occupying ourselves with a harmless and kind activity, namely the practice of meditation. Right effort is the balanced effort with which we observe and register, as a subtle support to being mindful. From this arises and grows the power of right mindfulness. As a direct result of a moment of mindfulness, we develop a deeper, natural focus on the experiences we are aware of. From right concentration deeper forms of right or clear insight are revealed. This automatically reinforces inner discipline and ethical sensitivity. Energy and effort increase and become more balanced with right mindfulness, concentration in turn becomes sharper, right view or understanding is deepening again, and so on.

Just like the five powers mentioned in the previous chapter, the aspects of the Eightfold Path are developed more and more. The Buddha compared this process to a wheel with eight spokes; this wheel is set in motion by the practice of meditation, and runs smoother and smoother as we continue to practise. In doing so we pass through the forms of insight outlined above, until the highest liberating insight is realised, crowning the process of meditation.

All these forms of insight are not theoretical or intellectual, but intuitive in nature. This wisdom proves to be very useful in daily life, therefore it can be seen as a valuable friend. It offers protection and thereby freedom from being (further) controlled by mental forces like desire, hatred and ignorance, which might otherwise overpower us. It is the key to self-knowledge, to how we can use skilful means to achieve desired results, and to how we can manage the ups and downs of life in a wise and skilful manner.

Wisdom works preventatively, because intuitively we can pick up signs of possible danger more easily, and we begin to understand how we may prevent, get round or creatively solve problems. In short, intuitive wisdom leads to happiness, the happiness of harmony and inner freedom.

NOTES

1. In the next chapter I will refer in detail to this healing aspect of insight meditation.

2. For more information about the experience of enlightenment and about *magga* and *phala* see chapter 14, and chapter 15 in the section 'Māra's Eighth Army'.

3. It is also said, however, that this process can happen so quickly that some meditators only realise much later that something has changed in their lives and that they experience more inner freedom.

13

SEVEN STAGES OF PURIFICATION

The practice of *vipassanā* meditation can be compared to the cultivation of a vineyard. A gardener will create space by getting rid of the weeds, taking care that the weeds will not come back. And he will make sure the plants get enough water, he will prune them, he will pick the ripe grapes, and so on. In *vipassanā* meditation mindfulness has the function of the gardener. Through consistent or regular care the fruits of liberating insight can come to maturity and be picked.

In order to effect this regularity, a daily – or in any case a regular – meditation practice is important. I have given some practical advice about this in chapter 10 (in the section 'Meditation in Daily Life'). And if we are also motivated to access deeper levels in the meditation process in a short time, it is definitely recommended to participate in retreats. When we devote a whole day, a weekend or an intensive retreat of seven or ten days to the practice of insight meditation, the five healing powers mentioned in chapter 11 can unfold more quickly and more effectively.

This process can be compared to making a fire before the invention of matches or lighters. A twig was rolled between both hands, one end resting on a small block of wood, for as long as was needed to develop enough heat through friction to create a spark. If this process was stopped prematurely, the heat that was developed lasted for a short while, but the twig and wood cooled easily. Then the whole process needed to be started again in order to create the right amount of friction. A longer or more intensive period of meditation can be seen as creating the necessary friction or heat. This will kindle the fire of insight.

Fire is known for its purifying properties. Practising insight meditation intensively has a comparable purifying effect, which is running parallel to the cultivation of the various forms of wisdom, as discussed in the previous chapter. Step by step all kinds of physical, mental and emotional purification processes take place as a result of more continuity in the mindfulness and a deepening of insight.

In Buddhist psychology seven of these purification processes are mentioned; in this chapter I would like to describe and explain these fruits of meditation briefly.

1. PURIFICATION OF OUR ETHICAL UNDERSTANDING, AND OF A CAREFUL INNER DISCIPLINE

Following ethical guidelines is extremely important as a foundation for walking a spiritual path in a balanced manner and for the practice of meditation. In chapter 4 I have discussed the subject of ethics in some detail, describing five fundamental precepts or guidelines. These are:

1. The advice not to kill
2. The advice not to steal
3. The advice to refrain from sexual conduct that is violent or abusive
4. The advice not to tell lies
5. The advice not to use alcohol and drugs to the extent that they cloud the mind and cause physical, mental, emotional or social damage

These elementary ethical guidelines protect us from the (unnecessary) painful consequences of unwholesome or unskilful actions.

When protected like this we are not plagued by feelings of guilt and remorse all the time, and we lay the foundation for a harmonious and effective meditation practice. Through the practice of meditation this ethical understanding is being developed (further) in a very natural way, because we become more sensitive to and more aware of our behavioural patterns and their consequences.

In addition, ethical lapses and errors – and we all know them to a greater or lesser extent – are purified or burnt clean. During a retreat we live in an environment that is low in sensual input, so we are less absorbed by or sucked into thoughts, emotions and sensory impressions. Mistakes and lapses from the past can easily surface. With acceptance and compassion we can name or note these memories of previous errors when they become predominant (of their own accord), and the accompanying feelings of shame, guilt or remorse. This in itself can be seen as a process of resolution and mourning. Such a process creates spaciousness and has a purifying and liberating effect: feelings of guilt, remorse and regret are burnt clean by mindfulness.

As a natural result of greater ethical sensitivity, and following on from refining the elaborated ethics as discussed in chapter 7, there is another form of morality, namely the careful discipline of protecting the senses (*indriya samvara sila*). In *vipassanā* meditation this means protecting – in a caring and subtle way – the six senses (and protecting ourselves from being conditioned by them): eyes, ears, nose, tongue, body and mind. This protection is achieved first of all by striving for a healthy balance in meeting our daily basic needs like eating, drinking and resting. We make sure these basic needs are met, without falling into extremes.

During an intensive meditation retreat we can extend this sensory protection by committing ourselves to look around as little as possible, and to keep our gaze down a few metres ahead of us in the walking meditation or during daily activities. The advantage of this is that we do not involve ourselves unnecessarily with other things or people. Usually it is recommended not to read or write on a retreat and to speak as little as possible (preferably only, if necessary, with the organiser or with the teacher).

On a deeper level, this so-called refraining of the senses will also involve choosing not to indulge in the sensory impulses we experience during meditation, but to see them merely as a meditation object. We observe and note them as 'hearing', 'hearing'; 'seeing', 'seeing'; 'smelling', 'smelling'; 'tasting', 'tasting'; 'touching', 'touching'; 'thinking', 'thinking'. Or when we become aware that we like what we see or hear or taste, we can note 'liking'. We do not push the experience away. Sensory stimuli don't need to be seen as an enemy or as a distraction, but instead we integrate them by using them as meditation objects. This inner discipline can be compared to the constant and loving care and alertness with which a mother hen protects and raises her chicks. The meditation process is protected against needless disturbances, distractions, and obstacles through this careful inner discipline and its purification. In this way the five healing powers of chapter 11 can safely be cultivated.

2. PURIFICATION OF EMOTIONS AND PURIFICATION OF THE MIND

As a natural outcome of the careful ethical protection and inner discipline, purification of emotions, and purification of the mind, will slowly but surely be realised.

This purification too has several aspects. First of all everyday hindrances or mental disturbances like desire, irritation, worry and anxiety, will no longer arise as much. This is a result of the sensory protection in the first purification. Mindfulness becomes more developed, and we can be in touch with the here and now much better. The conditionings and reactivity that normally happen quite easily now have fewer chances to come up, and our consciousness is less coloured.

Yet during a retreat we will notice that a number of reaction patterns can manifest themselves quite easily. In Buddhist psychology these patterns are called *nivaranas*. In chapter 8 I have already listed the traditional five *nivaranas*. Below I will enumerate them again, but I have added different facets of the same energy.

1. Sensory cherishing or desire; attachment in relation to what is seen, heard, smelt, tasted, touched or thought.
2. Irritation and other aspects like displeasure, resistance, impatience, anger, aggression, hatred, jealousy or miserliness.
3. Laziness, dullness, sleepiness, lethargy or tiredness.
4. Restlessness and worry, with its variants of excitement, agitation, fear, remorse or feelings of guilt.
5. Doubt, uncertainties, insecurity, mistrust, confusion, hesitation or indecisiveness.

In daily life these emotions can prevent us from functioning well, and they often create problems. In meditation too, they can cause frustration, particularly at times when we cannot cope with them in a skilful manner. In such moments we let ourselves be carried away by them and we forget what we are doing. At other times they are experienced as threatening, and we try to suppress them, and we cannot note this clearly either. This is why these emotions are called *nivarana* in Buddhist psychology, literally meaning 'hindrance'.

The healing power of mindfulness is largely the result of its friendly and compassionate character. We don't need to try to change our experience or to fight it, but we can learn to accept such emotions and to integrate them as a meditation experience. In this way resistance, desire, fear and laziness become just as valuable as feelings of joy, or the rising and falling of the abdomen. These experiences are a useful meditation teacher instead of a hostile hindrance.

In the same way we can lovingly integrate our defence mechanisms, like suppressing or rationalising emotions, projecting or denying – or the tendency to do this – into our meditation process as well.

When one of these mental states or defence mechanisms is clearly recognised in an accepting way and named or noted, an inner purification takes place, because in that moment there is no attachment, aversion or delusion. By noting – without preference and without aversion – what is presenting itself here and now, there is no longer attachment to that object, and it has become just an objectively perceived experience. For that moment there is no anger or resistance either, and finally there is no ignorance as regards what is happening either, but there is clear understanding and awareness of what is happening. In this way hindrances and defence mechanisms are transformed into rewarding and valuable meditation objects, and the mind is purified.

Therapeutically speaking, a purification process takes place as well. Because our mind is not consuming all kinds of new sensory impressions during meditation, unresolved emotional or psychosomatic problems – that we all carry with us – can gradually come to the surface. Often such problems are manifested in the form of physical tension or pain in the shoulders, the back or the stomach, or as headaches. Sometimes the meditator experiences strong feelings of nausea, and he or she can even become temporarily ill. These blockages can often express themselves as feelings of frustration, sadness, gloom, disappointment or fear.

In fact this is a healthy sign, because it signifies that a process of purification is taking place. Sogyal Rinpoche, a well-known Tibetan meditation teacher, once compared this process to washing dirty socks. When we put them in hot soapy water, initially rather smelly fumes will rise up from the water. If we simply continue to wash and rinse them, the smell will disappear and the socks will become clean.

It is the same with unresolved psychosomatic problems or tensions that can arise like fumes during the meditation process. By accepting and gently integrating them as meditation experiences, they no longer fester unconsciously or subconsciously. When we observe and register them objectively they lose their power, and old wounds can slowly heal or close. And if certain problems – for example physical complaints – don't disappear or cannot be healed, mindfulness will at least leave us less at their mercy. As a direct result of observing and noting pain with acceptance, and our emotional reactions to it, we create a subtle inner spaciousness or freedom, and the problems lose some of their psychological and emotional control and tyranny over us. In this way the purification of emotions and of the mind is realised.

3. PURIFICATION OF THE CONCEPT THAT THERE IS A 'SELF'

This purification comes about when our meditation process has progressed somewhat, and when the first stages of purification are already fully at work. There is greater continuity in moment-to-moment mindfulness, and the meditator experiences fewer long gaps or periods of not knowing what is happening in the here and now. Every moment that movements of the belly, physical feelings, thoughts, emotions, sounds and the like become clear, they are noted as long as they are predominant.

Mostly we are not fully aware of what is taking place here and now, so that from our childhood onwards, we have a rather hazy idea about reality. Through unconsciousness and through inaccurate observation we have the tendency to interpret our experience as 'self' or as 'mine'.

Look for instance at small children. They are given some toys and immediately these are considered as 'my car' or 'my doll'. This identification is usually quite strong, and it does not only express itself in the subjective perception of external objects, but also in relation to internal phenomena, like the body, sensory objects, thoughts, physical feelings and emotions. These experiences are therefore often (unconsciously) interpreted as '*my* body', '*my* thought', '*my* feeling', and so on.

Because we identify with all these experiences we are afraid to lose them, and we become sad when the experiences or objects with which we identified, disappear or diminish. Besides, it becomes much more difficult to cope with feelings of pain and discomfort, because they are seen as a hostile attack on '*my* leg' or '*my* back'.

According to Buddhist psychology this mechanism of identification is in fact a deep-rooted, unconscious mistake or a veiling of reality. In truth, there is no 'I' at all, but only a series of successive experiences. It can be compared to a fluorescent light: from a distance it seems as if the light is burning continuously, whereas in reality electricity is flickering on and off or shooting back and forth, each impulse having a beginning and an end.

Therefore we are always advised to note thoughts, feelings and other meditation experiences objectively, not as '*my* pain' but as 'pain', 'pain', 'thinking', 'thinking', etc. When we are noting moments of seeing, hearing, smelling and so on, and when at this time thoughts arise – for example the thought 'this is my knee', when we are looking at the knee – then such thoughts can be noted as 'thinking', 'thinking' or as 'interpreting', 'interpreting'. Ideas or judgements about ourselves or about our relationship with the world can be noted the moment we recognise them.

In this way every moment of acceptingly but at the same time objectively noting, removes the (unconsciously built up) patterns of identification. In that moment there is non-identification. The illusion of 'self' or 'mine' is broken because there is no dualism, nor is there a clouding of the natural flow of appearing and disappearing experiences.

This results in inner freedom, comparable to leaving behind unwanted baggage during a long trek. This freedom can be reinforced during retreats by also beginning to note the intentions before actions. In this way the intention to walk, to sit or to go to the toilet can be noted as 'intending', 'intending'. When this is cultivated more, the illusion that there is an 'I', 'you', 'he' or 'she' who is meditating, loses its power. In conventional terms we can say there is an 'I' or 'you', but in the ultimate sense there is only a process of cause and effect in bodily and mental phenomena. There is simply observing and noting, no more than that. In this sense *vipassanā* meditation is very scientific in nature, and there is objectivity as regards all our experience.

4. PURIFICATION BY TRANSCENDING DOUBT

Overcoming or transcending doubt and scepticism is a purifying process that comes about on the basis of the previous purification. The meditation practice becomes easier, and can be compared to a steam train, where the engine – after a difficult start with high fuel consumption – begins to run more smoothly all the time. In the same way the meditator finds it easier to observe and name or note that which is predominant in the moment. Intuitively we recognise the law of cause and effect in the mental and physical processes we are aware of. An example is how a sound can lead to thoughts, and thoughts in turn result in emotions that may sometimes be very powerful. Or how a physical sensation can give rise to awareness of it, and this may lead to worry, which then creates tension in the body. In this way we become more and more aware of these processes of cause and effect.

Gradually the understanding unfolds that there is no governing power or person behind these processes, but that it is merely a series of physical and mental activities. There is 'no self, no other' which is also the title of the Dutch translation of the book *Being Nobody, Going Nowhere* by the late Buddhist nun Ayya Khema from Germany.

In a non-intellectual manner we become aware of the appearance and disappearance of mental and physical phenomena in the here and now. We also become aware of how this process is being sustained and influenced by the law of cause and effect, by thoughts, food, and by our physical environment (e.g. weather conditions).[1] This gives us a deeper sense of reality, and in that moment a number of doubts are cleared up like doubt about what is wholesome and what is unwholesome, and doubts about the benefits of practising meditation. And we no longer doubt the illusory nature of ideas about the future.

This purification is reinforced by the recognition of the impermanence of all experience, which is becoming clearer at times. At this level, emotions, thoughts or physical sensations that we have been observing and registering (for some time) may suddenly disappear spontaneously. Without trying to 'note them away' they unexpectedly dissolve by themselves. Experiences like this give us confidence: we know we are on the right path, and that they are the fruit of our meditation practice. In this way the purification by transcending doubt is realised, which creates freedom and spaciousness.

5. PURIFICATION BY KNOWLEDGE AND VISION OF 'WHAT IS THE PATH AND WHAT IS NOT THE PATH'

During a retreat the powers of confidence, balanced effort, mindfulness, (momentary) concentration and insight are increasing, and there is more continuity in our observation. As indicated above, a new process of awareness is gradually unfolding: we begin to see more and more clearly how all experience is finite and transient. This impermanence is manifested during a very clear phase in our meditation practice, as the arising and passing away of meditation objects becomes quite obvious. We become aware of how and when thoughts, emotions, physical sensations and the like arise; we note them, and we watch them disappear of their own accord. Sometimes mindfulness is so sharp that the impulse of thoughts to arise is even recognised, which means that they already become extinguished in that moment.

This is the time when for longer or shorter periods, many meditators fall into a trap. Previously there were many unpleasant emotions, thoughts, pain, discomfort and fuzziness to deal with. Now this has suddenly changed. In the Buddhist scriptures ten possible experiences are described, so-called *upakilesa*. These *upakilesa* manifest themselves as follows:

1. We might see overwhelmingly beautiful colours or lights.
2. We obtain clear insight into the way we function, and into the nature of things.
3. We experience intense feelings of rapture, sometimes accompanied by bodily sensations like goose pimples, heat, pleasant vibrations, feelings of softness or lightness that can be so strong that sometimes it feels as though we are levitating.
4. We experience deep feelings of serenity, relaxation and calmness.
5. We may begin to feel blissful or satisfied.
6. We feel great confidence in ourselves and in the Dhamma; we are deeply touched by it. We experience feelings of gratitude, and we are determined to continue the practice, or we wish to convert others to the practice of meditation.
7. Sparkling energy wells up. This is expressed in feelings of strength, freshness, health, inspiration and motivation to meditate. The world is at our feet.
8. We experience great clarity of mind.
9. We may experience great equanimity and stability of mind, so that we view all appearing and disappearing objects objectively and in a harmonious way.
10. We feel attachment to and identification with one or more of these pleasant experiences.

These experiences are extremely pleasant and beautiful, and in many religious traditions they are seen as the final goal of the spiritual journey. The lights, for instance, can be interpreted as the divine light; the profound happiness as divine bliss. In *vipassanā* meditation however, these experiences are not viewed as the end of the path, and they are even called pitfalls or 'defilements of insight', the literal translation of the Pali term *upakilesa*. This is mainly due to the tenth *upakilesa*, attachment. Because of this attachment we lose our down-to-earth objectivity; in fact we are content with silver, while if we dug deeper we might find diamonds. Unconsciously at that moment we choose a subtle form of bondage. This becomes particularly obvious when the beautiful emotions disappear again. As a result we feel an enormous emptiness, and we miss something, comparable in some sense to the feelings of emptiness we may experience when we don't see our loved one for some time.

Often meditators who suffer from being blinded by the *upakilesa* are also more inclined to escape in daily life. Because in our everyday lives there are all kinds of difficulties and obstacles and as a meditator we would prefer to run back to that profound peace of the meditation, instead of trying to solve the problem skilfully. Therefore these pleasant experiences can create a duality when we don't integrate them as meditation objects.

However, because they can feel so overwhelming and blissful, we would like to keep them with us (preferably forever). Therefore we stop naming or we name in an inaccurate manner, in order to wallow in the emotion. There often is laziness at that moment and unknowingly we begin to identify with our experience. Some people also think they are enlightened for that moment, or they desire more pleasant experiences. Pride and conceit can easily arise.

The *upakilesa* influence can be compared to the attraction the heavenly songs of the deceitful Sirens had on Ulysses. Meditation teachers often face a difficult task when dealing with this. It can be quite some time before meditators realise that it is just a temporary phase in their meditation process, and that the beautiful experiences are not more important or of more value than pain, impatience, hearing a sound, thinking about the future, and the like. The moment this is fully understood and the pleasant experience is consistently integrated as a meditation object, we experience a more profound equilibrium, and it can be said that the fifth purification has been realised. We have seen through the deceptive heavenly songs of the beautiful experiences, and the knowledge of what is the path of meditation and what is not, is realised. The five *indriya* of chapter 11 are bundled more and more into powerful purifying forces.

6. PURIFICATION BY INTUITIVE KNOWLEDGE AND VISION OF THE WAY

When the previous purification has become sufficiently matured, then suddenly another difficult phase in the meditation process can occur. The experiences here can be quite overpowering, and sometimes they are so strong that we may consider stopping our practice altogether. In Burma this is sometimes called 'the stage of rolling up the mat'. Experiences that may occur during this time are:

- Intense fear or terror. We feel unstable, mentally ill and sometimes we are literally shaking.
- Strong feelings of gloom and depression. Physically we may feel weak, tired and heavy.
- Feelings of disgust and repulsion. Noting happens effortlessly, but we don't take any pleasure in it. We want to run away and go home.
- A deep sense of the suffering of the world.

- A strong wish to transcend the pain and the suffering. This makes us suddenly quite motivated and inspired to continue to practise. We become heated, agitated and excited.
- Intense physical pains and sensations, as if spears pierce our body, as if our body is being pulled apart, as if needles are being stuck into our back, and so on.

We have a tendency to interpret these experiences as negative; we might get the idea that we are doing something wrong in our practice. But in fact it is a sign that our practice is working and that purification is taking place. Now we get in touch with the three universal characteristics of impermanence, unsatisfactoriness and uncontrollability at a much deeper level. In the previous chapter I have already described these characteristics briefly. During our meditation practice we may experience them as follows:

1. Impermanence (*anicca*). Everything we observe arises, stays for some time, and falls away again. Sometimes this happens so quickly that we do not even have time to name phenomena separately. We can only stay in the present moment by noting the phenomena as a whole as 'knowing', 'knowing', 'chaos', 'chaos' and the like, instead of noting all the objects that are disappearing so quickly one by one. Even the rising and the falling of the abdomen seems very changeable; sometimes they happen quickly, at other times slowly; at times as a flowing movement, other times in stages, etc. They are never the same but always with a new beginning and ending.

2. Unsatisfactoriness (*dukkha*). Sometimes we experience immediate or obvious forms of suffering, such as physical pain or unpleasant emotions. Even moments of agreeable or neutral experiences are seen as unsatisfactory, because they are transient. They disappear again, we cannot rely on them in the long run, and if we can-

not deal with them skilfully they will result in new conditionings, like attachment, fear or sorrow. In this sense a continuous care and accuracy is needed in working with the burden of life. In all these transient experiences a true, everlasting peace can never be found.

3. Uncontrollability, ungovernability (*anattā*). Whether we like it or not, we sometimes have painful sensations or thoughts that we do not want at all at that moment. Or we experience something that is pleasant, and even though we want it to continue, sooner or later it falls away again. What is offered on our meditation plate is always a big surprise. The only thing we can do as a meditator is to observe and note all these unpredictable, ungovernable mental and physical processes.

In this sixth stage of purification, which runs parallel to the existential insight described in the previous chapter, we get in touch with these three realities in a profound way. Not by thinking about them, but by means of and as a result of direct observation. We might have a sense of this in our everyday lives, but usually it is quite snowed under, or not based on direct experience.

This stage of purification is very liberating in the sense that illusions we might unconsciously cherish, and unrealistic expectations we may have of (experiences in) life, are being burnt clean. Furthermore, gradually clear insight arises, supporting us to deal intuitively with the ups and downs of life in an easier way. Our tolerance in relation to painful and suffering experiences increases. We become like a rock in the surf. The sea may be quite peaceful and calm, or very rough, but the rock stays the same. It does not get scared, it doesn't need to escape or to fight, and it does not need to cling to anything, it is just there as it is. A mind that knows insight becomes just as stable and balanced.

After the painful and uncomfortable phase described above, suddenly everything becomes calm again. In this stage of the practice mindfulness and insight are mature and strong, the process unfolds by itself. Strong equanimity in noting the objects is typical of this stage. Meditation becomes easier, there is little pain, we can walk and sit for longer periods without much effort, and the mindfulness is very sharp and detailed.

Of course we might get stuck in this level of the practice as well. This may be caused by a subtle blindness as regards one or more of the defilements of insight, or because the five powers or *indriyas* are no longer in balance. So even at this level guidance from a teacher remains very important.

7. PURIFICATION BY INTUITIVE KNOWLEDGE AND INSIGHT

When meditative insight is profound and mature enough, and when the meditator and the situation are ready, the last purification may take place, namely the purification by intuitive knowledge and vision in relation to the experience of enlightenment or *nibbāna*. This seventh stage of the purification process can be seen as the *summum bonum* of mystical wisdom and liberation. In the next chapter I will elaborate on this highest fruit of insight meditation practice.

NOTES

1. These four are called the four *āhāras* or nutriments necessary for life.

14

ENLIGHTENMENT

In Buddhism, the experience of enlightenment is viewed as the ultimate happiness, and the final goal of the Eightfold Path. It is the realisation of the third noble truth: the truth of the cessation of suffering. In chapters 3 and 12 I have already touched on the experience of enlightenment or *nibbāna*. It is described as unconditioned and supramundane or transcendent in nature, and in no way connected with the everyday mental and physical phenomena that we know. It is experienced as the highest form of inner freedom.

This experience of enlightenment is not permanent. It is like seeing the sun for a short moment on a cloudy day. We see the sun in a flash, and the next moment the clouds have closed in again. But according to the Buddha and to meditators who have had this experience, this glimpse is permanent in the sense that forces we found difficult to manage and which were causing us problems are in that moment completely extinguished.

FOUR STAGES OF ENLIGHTENMENT

According to the *Theravāda* texts the mind of the meditator is purified in four stages, just like a house that is being cleaned in four days. First the basement, then part of the living room, then the rest of the living area and finally the attic.

1. The first stage is that of 'streamwinner' or *sotāpanna*. This is the term used to describe someone who has for the first time experienced an enlightened moment. The stream of conditioned experience has been broken for the first time. With this moment of realisation three destructive or difficult (if we do not deal with them wisely) tendencies or driving forces (*samyojanas*) are totally uprooted and extinguished[1] in that person. These forces are:

- Ego or sense of self. The belief – which is not based on reality – in a solid, substantial soul or self is completely eradicated. As a result, contraction and fear to lose that with which we identified before, disappear.

- Scepticism and doubts about reality and about our capacity for inner liberation no longer exist from that moment onwards. Confidence in the Buddha, the Dhamma and the Sangha and in the liberating power of meditation is unshakeable.

- Superstition disappears too. With superstition is meant the belief in rites and rituals without awareness of the underlying symbolism, and when they are engaged in on 'automatic pilot'. Merely carrying out the ceremony is already seen as purifying, and as a way to allay fears or to pacify a higher power; it does not really matter in which state of mind the action is done. These forms of superstition can be found in all religions. Examples are bathing in a particular river, making the sign of the cross, or prostrating in front of an image or statue with the idea that doing all these things *in and of themselves* are enough to purify the mind, to allay fears or to pacify higher powers. When doubt and uncertainty disappear, the fear of and the belief in a higher power – which we would need to pacify by means of rites and rituals – disappears as well.

It is said that a *sotāpanna* still has plenty of desire, attachment and hatred (and therefore is not a perfect goody-goody), but not to the extent that he or she will suffer greatly from these forces. And it is said about *sotāpannas* that they – karmically speaking – will be reborn a maximum of seven lifetimes within the conditioned cycle of birth and rebirth,[2] and that they are naturally inclined to reach higher stages of enlightenment within that time span.

2. The second stage of enlightenment is called that of the 'once-returner' or *sakadāgāmi*. When *nibbāna* is contacted for the second time, sensual desire and (the tendency to have) feelings of hatred, jealousy and miserliness are greatly reduced. These driving forces are not extinguished altogether but they become considerably weaker. The name indicates that a *sakadāgāmi* karmically speaking has one more life left to be fully liberated from all worldly conditionings.

3. The 'non-returner' or *anāgāmi* is somebody who spiritually speaking has reached deeper levels. At a third enlightenment experience (the tendency to have) sensual desire, hatred, miserliness and jealousy are completely extinguished. According to the scriptures, an *anāgāmi* is not reborn in the human realm and has at most one more life to live in an ethereal realm.

4. The 'fully purified one' or *arahat* has realised the highest stage of enlightenment. For the *arahat* all remaining subtle conditionings are extinguished as well: forms of attachment as regards meditative absorption, pride, restlessness and all other delusions as regards the reality of the here and now. It can be said that an *arahat* no longer has any mental problems, and that his or her mind has become as pure or as clear as a mirror. Dirt or dust from the environment can settle on the mirror, but is not absorbed by

it. *Arahats* no longer cause any physical, mental, emotional or social damage to themselves or to others.

Life might seem boring or flat after realising a purified mind like that. However, the ten *samyojanas* are replaced by a great spaciousness, creating room for wholesome forces to flourish, such as compassion, unconditional love and wisdom. Moments where otherwise we would be impatient or fearful can now be used in a totally different way. Such people are a shining light in a neurotic society.

According to the scriptures *arahats* continue to live as ordinary human beings until they die, and until that moment they may still be subject to the results of previous actions. However, they will not mentally suffer from these. Because of their complete purity of mind *arahats* do not commit actions that are karmic in nature and that create results in their consciousness. For them, the whole process of cause and effect stops at the moment of death and liberation has become complete.

HOW LONG DOES THIS PURIFICATON PROCESS TAKE?

In fact this question cannot really be answered; it depends on many factors. Some important aspects in this are motivation, intuition as regards understanding the principle of the meditation practice, the time spent practising, the degree of conditioning, health, and guidance received in the practice. The Buddha himself did not mention a standard timeframe within which someone can realise enlightenment. In the *Satipatthāna Sutta* (see also appendix 1) he made the following statement:

> *Bhikkhus, whoever has fully developed these four foundations of mindfulness for seven years, may expect one of two results: higher knowledge here and now, or, if there is still a remainder of clinging, the state of non-returner.*

When someone does not need seven years to fully develop these four foundations, but six years . . .
When someone does not need six years . . . but five years . . .
When someone does not need five years . . . but four years . . .
When someone does not need four years . . . but three years . . .
When someone does not need three years . . . but two years . . .
When someone does not need two years . . . but one year . . .
When someone does not need one year . . . but seven months . . .
When someone does not need seven months . . . but six months . . .
When someone does not need six months . . . but five months . . .
When someone does not need five months . . . but four months . . .
When someone does not need four months . . . but three months . . .
When someone does not need three months . . . but two months . . .
When someone does not need two months . . . but one month . . .
When someone does not need one month . . . but half a month . . .
When someone does not need half a month to develop these four foundations of mindfulness but seven days, then one of two results may be expected: highest knowledge here and now, or, if there is still a remainder of clinging, the state of non-returner.

So the meditation process can unfold quite quickly and easily. However, in practice I think that particularly for westerners more time is needed. Sometimes I turn the quotation around, and then it starts as follows:

When someone does not need seven days . . . but half a month . . .
When someone does not need half a month . . . but one month . . .
When someone does not need one month . . . but two months . . .
When someone does not need two months . . . but three months . . .
Etc.

In my mind I would go as far as seven lifetimes for myself and for many other (Western) meditators.

ENLIGHTENMENT CAN HAPPEN IN EVERY MOMENT?!

Ultimately it does not really matter how long we would need to practise before we can experience the happiness of *nibbāna*. What I have said above about enlightenment is not meant to make us strive for some ideal while neglecting our everyday experiences in the here and now. Because there is a very real danger that we identify with some ideal image of complete inner freedom and purified consciousness. And then, when forms of desire, hatred, aversion, doubt or other conditionings present themselves in the here and now we might be inclined to judge or suppress them. This would only cause us to get further removed from insight and inner freedom.

The explanation about the seven stages of purification is meant as an indication, and it describes the liberating and purifying character of *vipassanā* meditation. In all this the present moment should not be skipped over or neglected. Ultimately every moment of mindfulness is in fact already a moment of enlightenment, as the liberating antithesis of the dark and manipulative unconscious or subconscious.[3]

The moment something is recognised and noted, there is no identification and attachment with regard to the object of observation. There is no aversion either, because the meditation object is noted objectively. There is no ignorance either, but instead there is clear seeing or knowing of what is happening here and now. In the language of Zen Buddhism we could call it a moment of realising of our Buddha nature. We are in an oasis; a cool place that protects us from the dry, hot deserts of desire, hatred and delusion.

Any meditation object may be used to reach that oasis: rising, falling, hearing, thinking, feeling, but also anger, doubt, desire or fear. The moment anger, for example, is recognised and noted with acceptance, we are no longer *in* that anger. The anger might still be there, but at the same time some inner space has been created. The anger is observed and noted with a subtle distance, and the charge is taken out of it. In this way all kinds of mental and physical experiences can be used as fuel for (more and more) moments of abiding in the oasis of the present moment.

The Buddha once said that developing mindfulness through training in meditation is the most direct way to the happiness of self-knowledge, insight and inner freedom. Through *vipassanā* meditation we can learn to deal in a wise manner with pleasant and unpleasant experiences in life, identify less with them, and in this way realise more happiness and inner freedom. We learn to face and accept our moments of openness and purity, but also our blockages and subconscious thinking patterns and habits. By subsequently naming or noting them, a certain spaciousness or freedom is created; we are no longer *in* it, we are no longer ruled by them. In this way they slowly but surely lose their power. *Vipassanā* meditation can be seen as a very simple but at the same time profound way to realise more inner freedom.

Furthermore, in the practice of *vipassanā* meditation gradually more insight is developed into the impermanent, burdensome, afflictive and uncontrollable nature of life. This insight may culminate in the realisation of enlightenment, where – according to the Buddha and those who have walked this path – a transformation takes place in the mind, because emotions that we have difficulty dealing with, like desire, hatred, delusion, fear and doubt, are completely extinguished.

The Buddha compared the essence of his teachings once with the ocean. *Just like the ocean has one taste, the taste of salt, in the same way this teaching has one taste, the taste of freedom.*

NOTES

1. The literal translation of the term *nibbāna* is 'not (or no longer) blowing or burning'.

2. See chapter 6.

3. The well-known Swiss psychiatrist C. G. Jung beautifully formulated it as: *We do not become enlightened by imagining all kinds of radiant images, but rather by becoming aware of our own inner darkness.*

15

OBSTACLES ON THE PATH

In previous chapters the various fruits of the practice of insight meditation have been mentioned. We may, however, be faced with many obstacles and hindrances. The Buddha classified a number of these obstacles in what has been called 'The Ten Armies of Māra.' Māra is the slayer of virtue and the destroyer of wholesome living. Māra can be seen as the Buddhist alternative to Satan and symbolises all kinds of temptations arising in the meditation practice.

In the *Sutta Nipāta* the Buddha mentioned ten different armies of Māra:

1. Sensual pleasure and attachment (*kāma*)
2. Discontent (*arati*)
3. Hunger and thirst (*khuppipāsā*)
4. Craving (*tanhā*)
5. Laziness and drowsiness (*thina-middha*)
6. Fear (*bhiru*)
7. Doubt (*vicikicchā*)
8. Hypocrisy and conceit (*makkha* and *thambha*)
9. Gain, fame and praise (*lābha, siloka* and *sakkāra*)
10. Arrogance and the demeaning of others (*attukkamsana* and *paravambhana*)

In this chapter these ten armies will be discussed separately.

1. SENSUAL PLEASURE AND ATTACHMENT

This means primarily that we take pleasure in what we see, hear, smell, taste, touch or think. At that time the dispassionate and objective observation process has stopped and there can be no deepening of insight. Only at the moment we recognise and note this enjoying or cherishing as such, can insight arise again. But it may take a long time for this enjoyment or cherishing to be recognised and noted; sometimes we completely forget to integrate it into the meditation process and to use it as an object of meditation. This means Māra's first army is overpowering us. My Burmese meditation teacher in Thailand, Achan Asabha, used to joke about meditators who were in retreat. While practising walking meditation they would look around casually and on seeing attractive men or women, they would stop the walking meditation and go over and talk to them, just like ants are attracted to sugar.

In the texts there is a story illustrating this about a monk who had every intention to spend the night in meditation on top of a mountain. There were sounds, smells and lights of the partying village below, and the monk became so overwhelmed by all these sense impressions that he eventually abandoned his meditation and went down to the village to join the crowds.

I do not mean to say that we are not allowed to enjoy, but rather that sensual pleasure is a temptation a meditator has to recognise in order to experience genuine deepening of the practice. That is why in a retreat we are advised to behave like a blind person (meaning not to look around) and like a deaf person (not to enter into conversations). In addition we are advised to note seeing, hearing, smelling, tasting, touching and thinking every time it arises, at the moment it happens. If we recognise a sound as car, bird or whatever, we note 'recognising' or 'interpreting'. When there is a thought or feeling of enjoying or clinging in relation to the sensual perception, we can note the thinking, the enjoying or the clinging again. In this way inner discipline and mindfulness act as a preventive and they 'restrain' sensual pleasure and clinging.

The first army of Māra can also manifest itself as attachment to a partner, children, relatives, possessions, work – for example our own business, or a job with many responsibilities – or friends. This causes daydreaming, wanting to write letters or make telephone calls, or wanting to go home to see if the children are all right. Here, too, attachment is tempting us to temporarily abandon or to stop altogether with the meditation practice. If we want to render this army harmless, it is advisable during a period of intensive meditation to make a strong commitment not to get caught up in these dreams, thoughts and feelings of desire, attachment, loneliness, fear, anxiety or responsibility. Instead we integrate all these consistently as meditation objects. In this way the first temptation can be overcome.

2. DISCONTENT

This temptation arises and increases when during a meditation retreat there is something not to our liking. Dissatisfaction or irritation can be caused by a variety of reasons, like a breakdown in communications between the meditation teacher and us. The environment where we are practising may cause dissatisfaction, because we think our room is too small or too noisy. We can't sleep at night because our neighbour is snoring. Or we feel that the atmosphere of the retreat is too strict or not inspiring enough to enable us to develop mindfulness. So there can be many causes for discontent.

In every situation, and particularly in Southeast Asian monasteries, there often are unexpected elements, and initially we interpret them as distractions. Some examples are listed below:

- There is a power cut.
- Coconuts fall with a terrible bang on the corrugated iron roof of our meditation hut.
- All day long pigeons climb and clatter on that same roof. The scratching sound of their feet is like the shrill sound of a piece of chalk on a blackboard.
- Young monks keep asking us to teach them English.
- We fall ill, which makes it impossible to follow the familiar meditation schedule.
- The translator or meditation teacher has suddenly left to go on holiday for a few days or even a week.
- The meditation centre is 'invaded' by curious visitors or by students from the local police academy, leaving no space in the meditation hall.
- We are asked to take part in a photo shoot or video reportage.
- In one particular retreat venue in the Netherlands, during the walking meditation, when all meditators are walking slowly to the dining room, they are cheered on by a group of teenage boys who are commenting on the 'race' and placing bets on who is going to win.

In fact these are interesting learning experiences because, whether we want to or not, we will be faced with unexpected and distracting situations throughout our lives. In normal everyday life we usually either try to push away those situations or we are totally controlled by them.

A meditation retreat is an excellent opportunity for learning to use unpleasant feelings and discontent as meditation objects instead of resisting them or being carried away by them and trying all kinds of complicated tricks to control them.

Of course there are limits. In Burma I suffered from an intestinal parasite for weeks and benefited not only from just noting it but also from getting good medical treatment. However, these are instructive situations challenging us to learn to set our limits in a wise manner when our meditation process is jeopardised. It can also teach us to be content with little and to deal skilfully with Māra's second army. This involves learning to walk the middle way between two extremes. On the one hand without suppressing feelings of dissatisfaction, on the other without being the slave of those feelings and giving in to them. Following this middle way means that unexpected situations and irritations are not suppressed or pursued, but lovingly accepted as objects of meditation. They are considered fertile soil for cultivating intuitive insight, for they show us directly the uncontrollable and unpredictable nature of existence, and they are opportunities to deepen our insight.

3. HUNGER AND THIRST

Hunger and thirst can cause specific temptation, particularly when our needs for food and drink are not being met in the retreat situation. Perhaps no coffee is served, whereas we are used to drinking coffee. Perhaps the Buddhist monastic rules are applied meaning there will be no food after twelve noon, or we realise our digestive system does not react well to the food being served at the retreat.

During a retreat food is very important and so it is always sensible to enquire beforehand about a particular diet or special types of food you are used to or need for medical reasons. If you think the food will not be right for you, bring some food along. There are limits, however. Keep it simple. It will be difficult to balance the retreat food perfectly for all your needs.

So in the area of eating and drinking, too, we are encouraged to walk the golden middle way and to look skilfully after our own basic needs. We should take sufficient food and liquids so that physically we can function well. Be careful not to go to the extremes of too much or too little. And the moment feelings of hunger or thirst arise in the meditation practice, we can observe these and note them as 'hunger', 'hunger', 'hunger' or as 'thirst', 'thirst', 'thirst'. It is also helpful to keep an eye on Māra's second army, discontent.

4. CRAVING

As a result of the first, second and third armies of Māra not being recognised clearly, desire can arise: mental grasping or craving for something we miss. This army can be obsessive and may express itself as the desire for food or liquids, for sensual or sexual pleasure or for a luxurious bed. On a more subtle level it manifests itself as the desire to experience thoughts, bodily sensations, sensual stimulation or emotions, or no longer wanting to experience them.

In Buddhism, craving is sometimes compared to the behaviour of a cock, for two reasons. Firstly because a cock has never enough to eat and secondly because cocks are often chasing chickens and can 'never get enough' of that either.

If desire is not dealt with skilfully it will easily give rise to attachment, and attachment makes us unfree and frustrated. Craving appears to be a driving force, not easily satisfied, and exhausting. Therefore it is seen in Buddhist psychology as the immediate cause of the suffering we experience as human beings.[1]

Denying, ignoring, suppressing and giving in are the most common ways we deal with desire. Whether in the long term these approaches will bring us enduring happiness and wisdom remains to be seen.

Through the practice of insight meditation we become familiar with a new approach. We learn to walk a path where we do not immediately give in to desires and needs nor do we suppress or deny them. And we learn to deal skilfully with desires, and to observe and note them simply as they are, for as long as they are clearly present.

We do the same with all forms of desire. As regards our everyday life the Buddha advised: To refrain from doing harm and to cultivate what is wholesome. But for the practice of insight meditation he gave the following words of advice which go beyond good and bad: To purify the mind. He referred to the karmically conditioned results of both unwholesome and wholesome desires when we are, consciously or unconsciously, controlled by them. Both forms of desire are conditioning us when we fail to recognise and integrate them as meditation objects into our practice. So in meditation practice we do not have to distinguish between wholesome or unwholesome wanting and craving. Even the desire for enlightenment, for doing wholesome actions or for experiencing or continuing to experience wholesome states of mind should be observed and noted, as they are, and as long as they are there.

Awareness is the key to learning to deal skilfully with desire. If we are not aware of or are only half-aware of desire, we will notice that we unwittingly become caught in Māra's net. It can be compared with the breakdown of a car. If we do not know what is wrong with the car, we cannot repair it. The moment the cause of the problem is recognised the car can be fixed.

In the same way we often suffer as the result of unknowingly being controlled by desire. Getting angry does not help; inner exploration does. We can see the practice of insight meditation as an inner investigation that gives us slowly and gradually more understanding of those previously unconscious forms and effects of desire.

We can also pay attention to how desire can be prevented from arising. Buddhist psychology states that desire is a direct result of not observing or not paying close attention to physical and/or mental feelings. The moment we hear, see, smell, taste, touch, think or experience something, a pleasant, unpleasant or neutral feeling arises simultaneously.[2] If these feelings are not clearly recognised and noted they can easily cause desire. When the feelings are pleasant, there is the desire to keep that feeling or situation or to experience it again; with unpleasant feelings the desire to end that sensation or situation or to get rid of it arises. Unrecognised neutral feelings easily cause confusion, doubt, restlessness or boredom. When these emotions are not clearly recognised they in turn cause desire for clarity, security, calmness or feeling more obvious or stronger sensations.

So developing mindfulness of pleasant, unpleasant and neutral feelings as soon as they become clear to us helps to prevent desire from arising by depriving it of the fuel to develop. And even when desire does arise, then this desire can be used as an object of meditation.

It is good to realise that we need not judge or condemn desire.[3] A pitfall that is often overlooked in dealing skilfully with desire is that we have the tendency to judge the experience of desire negatively. I remember having this tendency myself when I started meditating. Such a negative attitude towards desire may be rooted in our upbringing ('thou shall not covet') or can arise when we read or hear that meditation practice will bring detachment. Mindfulness, however, is always accepting and non-idealistic. So we do not have to see desire as our enemy or as something that is not allowed. Rather we can gratefully integrate it as a meditation object into our practice.

We need not try to let go of desire or attachment in our meditation practice. When we observe desire and the resulting attachment with acceptance, and name or note it as 'desire', 'desire', 'attachment', 'attachment', 'wishing', 'wanting', 'not wanting', 'resistance', 'aversion' and the like, already in that moment a subtle inner detachment happens. In that moment we are no longer *in* the desire; it has been objectified. There is non-identification in relation to the experience of desire. In this way desire and attachment can be used as valuable objects of awareness and noting, every moment they are clearly present. The fourth army of Māra can be transformed and incorporated into the 'liberation forces of *vipassanā* meditation'.

5. LAZINESS AND DROWSINESS

For many practitioners drowsiness is the biggest obstacle in their meditation practice, and I was also struggling with this for a long time. In the West, sleepiness is often seen from a psychological perspective as resistance, not wanting – consciously or unconsciously – to feel pain or grief and therefore sinking into sleepiness.

This may be so but is not always the case. Sleepiness can also indicate lack of sleep, mental fatigue and boredom. It can also arise after having eaten or because of an imbalance between effort and concentration.[4] This imbalance can happen for various reasons:

- Pleasant experiences are not noted or not noted carefully enough, causing first lethargy or laziness and then dullness in the mind.
- In sitting meditation more concentration is developed naturally, whereas in the walking meditation more energy or effort is developed. Mindfulness is the central factor in both walking and sitting meditation; it is only the supporting factors that have different aspects. That is why as a rule it is advised in meditation retreats to walk for the same length of time as to sit. But many practitioners prefer the sitting meditation or consider it more important than the walking, thereby unconsciously strengthening the concentration factor and losing effort or energy. This weakens and dulls the mindfulness and so concentration becomes predominant, causing us to sink into our observations without knowing it, which makes us dull and sleepy.

- Individual tendencies play a part too. Some people develop a strong concentration quite naturally. This can show itself in the inclination towards sleepiness in the meditation.

Whatever the cause, sleepiness remains a difficult meditation object, especially because it is so difficult to be aware of it. So I will give a few practical suggestions.

1. See laziness, dullness and sleepiness not as enemies but as a kind of '*vipassanā* flu'. Just as with the flu it is better not to force yourself but to take some extra care of yourself and your symptoms; in this case you care for the sleepiness and integrate it as a valuable meditation object. See it as a challenge to accept feeling sleepy as a meditation object on the one hand, and on the other hand you try to name and note it when it is predominant. In this way you can observe and note or name laziness, dullness, sleepiness, lethargy and the light, 'woolly', heavy or tired feeling as a meditation experience. When you are yawning, the swaying or falling forward of the body when you actually do fall asleep for a moment, or whatever symptoms of the *vipassanā* flu are predominant, all these can be used and noted as meditation objects.

2. If despite having followed the advice of the first suggestion for a while, you get sucked deeper into sleepiness, you can use one or more of the following strategies:

- Start rubbing your head and neck slowly for some time with your hands while observing and noting the movements, giving yourself some extra sensations.
- Note the intention to open your eyes and then open them with mindfulness. Note the seeing, and practise for a while with your eyes open, keeping your gaze down a few metres in front of you. When your eyes begin to feel heavy, you can note that.

- Look with mindfulness at the sun or into a source of artificial light.
- Change your posture, stand up for a while or practise walking meditation. When sleepiness occurs often it is advisable to practise the walking meditation five or ten minutes longer than the sitting meditation during these periods of drowsiness.
- Be moderate in eating. This is helpful when you feel very sleepy after a meal.
- If you get sleepy during walking meditation, walk backwards or go back to a less complicated walking exercise.
- When you are extremely tired take a nap after a meal during the first few days of the meditation retreat.

3. If all of the above fails and sleepiness is still there, then just sit with it. When you fall asleep in the sitting you will notice you wake up again. It is not disastrous to fall asleep; a short 'meditation nap' can be very refreshing and you can see it as recharging the 'energy battery'.

According to Buddhist texts sleepiness and dullness are only overcome completely at the realisation of the highest stage of enlightenment. So it is a persistent army and requires patience and creativity to learn to handle and overcome it.

6. FEAR

Fear, too, can create quite a barrier, when we are totally in it and controlled by it, or when we completely dismiss or deny experiencing any feelings of fear. Fear has several causes:

- Sometimes we experience strong pain and/or unresolved emotions we have previously suppressed. Being faced with these deeper pains, frustrations and mistakes may cause fear to arise, particularly if we are not ready or not yet ready to face them.

- We miss something or somebody we are attached to.
- We experience fear caused by deep feelings of insecurity, often rooted in childhood.
- We have weird meditation experiences such as strange images or fantasies, or physical phenomena like intense itching, heat, cold, strange convulsive movements or contractions that we never encountered before. During the practice we can also experience an altered awareness of the body, like becoming bigger or smaller, or sensing the disappearance of the body or part of the body. In fact these experiences clearly show the uncontrollability of everything; therefore they are valuable meditation phenomena. But not being familiar with them they can seem quite threatening.
- There may be unpleasant physical or mental sensations or feelings during the meditation practice that we do not fully understand. This may cause us to think we are not practising correctly. Not noting this doubt, or not noting it carefully enough, causes more feelings of fear.
- As we get more in touch with the three universal characteristics of impermanence, unsatisfactoriness and uncontrollability, feelings of fear, insecurity and instability may arise.

Whatever the reason, fear is a feeling or an emotion experienced by all meditators. Sometimes the feeling is manifested simply as fear or panic; sometimes physical symptoms like sweating, shaking, and a quickened heartbeat are predominant, or the rising and falling movement may become faster or occur higher up in the body.

Fear can also manifest itself on a more subtle level. It may show as anxiety or as resistance. Examples are repressing, rationalising, projecting or denying problems, like making jokes when feeling sad. These are survival strategies, often developed unconsciously, so that we remain unaware of fear, conflict or tension, or release them in some other way.[5]

Fear is a difficult emotion. For some people it can be useful to practise – besides *vipassanā* meditation – meditation on lovingkindness or another form of tranquillity meditation as an 'indirect' and supporting strategy in learning to deal with fear.[6] However, it is usually better not to practise these meditation methods during a period of insight meditation. In mixing the two practices we can easily fall into a trap: in difficult times we choose to escape to another form of meditation. At that moment we deny ourselves the opportunity to learn to integrate the difficult situation into the *vipassanā* meditation process and the progress of liberating insight will be impeded. Therefore the advice is to practise different meditation methods alongside each other and not together, not in the same session.

But practising tranquillity meditation regularly can gradually soften the recurring experience of fear and may gradually create a fundamental sense of safety and security, allowing *vipassanā* meditation to be practised more easily.

If we are functioning quite well in our ordinary daily life, a 'direct' strategy can be applied. We no longer let ourselves be pushed by the fear of fear and we learn to recognise, accept and note fear as a meditation object, as it is and as long as it is clearly present. Sometimes fear expresses itself physically, at other times it is manifested in emotions or as resistance.

It is sufficient to know there is fear, and whatever is prominent at that moment can be noted: sweating, heartbeat, worry, anxiety, vulnerability, mental instability, panic, suppressing, rationalising and so on. It is not necessary to look for explanations or to try to become calm; we also do not need to rationalise or judge our fear. If we notice that we are doing so, then this too can be noted as 'rationalising', 'rationalising' or as 'judging', 'judging'.

Dealing with fear in this way does not always work immediately so we may sometimes experience quite difficult or fearful meditation sessions. It may help to frame or note the experiences differently. Instead of labelling the emotion as 'fear' we can note it as 'anxiety' or 'knowing' (that there is a difficult emotion). The burden of fear can get lighter by noting in this way.

It is also good to realise that we can stop the session at any time. However, just to keep following the discipline of sitting and walking usually proves to work best and to bear fruit eventually. We extend the limits of what we are willing to tolerate and we lose some fear of the fear. In due course we will discover naturally what is happening and learn to recognise and accept fear and the symptoms of fear. In that moment, fear becomes workable: we can note it and there is more spaciousness around it. Fear is objectified and thereby overcome.

Apart from this – if we don't feel well established in the practice of *vipassanā* meditation – it is often skilful not to discipline ourselves too much in daily life. When we notice that from an emotional point of view meditation practice is a burden in our life, we could try practising not more than 15–30 minutes every day instead of an hour, a whole day or several days on end.

Having interviews with a meditation teacher, and to share our meditation experiences regularly during evenings or days of group meditation, often provide great insights. We will be expected to be open and allowing, but if we have the courage to accept the experience of fear and so share it in a circle of people we are familiar with, it can turn into a source of insight, self-confidence and power.

7. DOUBT

Doubt easily arises when we feel we are not making progress in the practice, when we start thinking about the future or about what the practice can offer us. Doubt may also arise when we are frequently controlled or attacked by Māra's other armies. The tendency to doubt and to feel insecure may also be rooted in some way in our childhood (strict, judging parents or little moral support). Doubt can manifest itself in many different ways such as scepticism, indecisiveness, insecurity, mistrust, hopelessness, discouragement or despair. It can direct itself to the guidance during the retreat; we begin to wonder if the teacher is competent enough and whether he or she really understands us. Doubt can also express itself in uncertainty, for example not being sure whether we are practising correctly or whether we are just fooling ourselves. We begin to doubt whether we are not repressing anything. And we wonder if the powerful feelings of anger, fear, dejection, pain and discomfort that arise from time to time, or the many and sometimes ridiculous thoughts we have, will not drive us crazy.

Doubt usually arises when we start thinking about what we are doing. Buddhist psychology uses the term *ayoniso manasikāra*, 'an interpretation of the present moment that is not based on understanding'. So in order not to get caught up in doubt, it is important to note philosophical, analysing or rationalising thoughts as soon as they arise. Then doubts and associated emotions will come up less easily. And if they do arise we can integrate these as our meditation object, just like the other armies of Māra.

In addition to this, in the *Sammohavinodani* – an important commentary and text relating to the practice of mindfulness – some useful hints are given to help overcome doubt within and outside the meditation process:

- Do not hesitate to ask critical questions.
- Be open during the interviews and in sharing with meditation groups about what your concerns are. Make use of other people's wisdom and support.
- Do not harm yourself and others.
- Stick to the discipline during retreats even though at times you don't feel like it or you find it difficult.

- Do not stop a session of walking or sitting meditation before the predetermined time.
- Do not change posture during sitting meditation unnecessarily, unless the pain or discomfort becomes unbearable and you begin to force yourself.[7]
- Make friends with other meditators.
- Regularly join a meditation group and listen to Dhamma talks.
- Read books about the practice of meditation.

8. HYPOCRISY AND CONCEIT

The armies of hypocrisy and conceit usually arrive a little later, from the rear, and they also come in the guise of pride. They can manifest themselves as a quality of mind, but are also quite often a deluded response to the ideas we have about progress in our meditation practice. Particularly in the stage of progress where we experience pleasant and wholesome emotions[8], these armies may overpower us. We are satisfied with our practice and we become lazy. When the meditation teacher gives the down-to-earth advice just to note these pleasant experiences as well, in a consistent manner, we think this is nonsense and we only pretend to follow this advice. Of course we know better ourselves and we no longer need all this guidance and advice. The result is that we get stuck in the meditation process.

A different situation that can result in pride, hypocrisy or conceit sometimes happens when meditators think they have reached a higher stage of insight or enlightenment, while this is not the case. In chapter 12 the realisation of enlightenment or *nibbāna* is described as the succession of *magga* (the path) and *phala* (the fruit), two very subtle transcendent states of consciousness which follow one another as quickly as a flash of lightening and which uproot unwholesome states of mind.[9]

This experience is often called 'cessation'. For an instant the ordinary, worldly mental and physical processes disappear completely; there is a moment of ultimate emptiness. There are, however, many other reasons for such a moment of emptiness or 'disappearing'. In his book *Vipassanā-bhāvanā* the Thai meditation master and *Abhidhamma* scholar Dhanit Yupho mentions five causes:

- sleepiness (*thina-middha*)
- rapture (*piti*)
- profound peace of mind (*passaddhi*)
- concentration (*samādhi*)
- equanimity (*upekkhā*)

When these emotions or mental states are very strong, a moment of emptiness can sometimes be experienced. This emptiness is unconscious, however. In that moment there is no mindfulness and this experience has no real insight value. But meditators sometimes interpret these experiences as the realisation of ultimate emptiness through *magga-phala* while it was really no more than 'pseudo-enlightenment'. The confusion can become worse if a teacher insists that his or her student has realised a moment of enlightenment while this was not really what was happening.

This wrong interpretation of what really is just a moment of not being fully aware may result in conceit and can totally mislead somebody searching for wisdom. In some cases it can completely block his or her progress in the meditation.

Wise and skilful teachers will be very circumspect in explaining to their students the level of insight these students might have reached. Teachers don't want to burden us unnecessarily with knowledge that only leads to reactions of disappointment, conceit or desire, because we may start thinking we have nearly attained the full realisation of enlightenment.

The most skilful approach, according to them, is to leave it unspoken whether we have had an enlightened moment or not. As long as we notice that we still have obvious or latent feelings of hatred, pride or desire, there is reason enough just to continue the meditation practice. Simply observe and note whatever thoughts arise about whether or not there was the realisation of *magga-phala*; just use these thoughts as meditation objects and let them be.

9. GAIN, FAME AND PRAISE
10. ARROGANCE AND THE DEMEANING OF OTHERS

These last two armies of Māra may infiltrate and poison the mind of a successful meditation teacher. There are many examples of teachers, who are falling or who have fallen for the gifts they have received, or who have become intoxicated by fame, power and adulation. Then inner freedom will be hard to find. There is the danger that one gets more and more involved in showing and emphasising one's own purity, understanding and good qualities, while criticising other teachers or facilitators, and advising students not to get meditation instruction from other teachers. The result is an unhealthy, narrow presentation of the Dhamma and a deluded meditation teacher who is a bad example to others.

Māra's eighth army, too, may arise for meditation teachers. Because teachers are – often unconsciously – put on a pedestal by meditators, they may be tempted to show only the better aspects of themselves, and to hide or brush over dark or less enlightened aspects. The effects can be disappointing and sometimes dramatic when teachers turn out to be less holy than people thought, and fall off their pedestal. So honesty and openness are important virtues for meditation teachers, while for students it would be more beneficial if they dedicated themselves to realising the Dhamma. Guidance on the spiritual path is indispensable, but teachers are ultimately only showing the way. We can trust that most meditation teachers may indeed have more experience regarding the practice of meditation and are therefore good guides, but they are probably not fully enlightened yet and still have a lot to learn.

Whether we are just starting to meditate, have some more experience or are already teaching meditation, during the practice Māra's armies are forever ready to tempt us and to undermine our meditation process. The story of Prince Siddhattha illustrates this. He had found a suitable spot under a large tree and had resolved to stay sitting there until he had realised the highest wisdom about the attainment of happiness. He, too, was visited by Māra's tempting armies. The first came in the guise of beautiful, sensuous women. Then Māra came as voices speaking to the prince and asking why he was so stupid just to sit there navelgazing whereas he could have many beautiful women in his harem and be a powerful king. Next Māra came disguised as terrifying mental images, and as doubt. The *bodhisatta* wanted to end his quest for enlightenment, but then suddenly remembered he had vowed not to give up until he had gained true insight. It is said that he took some inner distance from these tempting forces and could recognise them as lust, fear and doubt. He touched the earth with his hand so it could be a witness to his aspirations and he said to himself: Māra, I know you. He did not condemn Māra, he did not suppress the emotions nor did he act on them. He simply acknowledged their presence, which caused Māra to withdraw.

When Māra's armies knock on our door we can remember this story and overcome these armies simply by using them, and integrating them as objects of observation and noting. Not only in the meditation practice but also in daily life, we can consider it as an extraordinary power and art to be free, and to remain free from the tempting and misleading forces of Māra. This brings calmness, peace, stability and inner freedom. The passage from the *Sutta Nipāta*, which was quoted at the beginning of this chapter, ends with the following words: Without courage Māra cannot be overcome, but when Māra has been overcome profound happiness is the result.

NOTES

1. See chapter 3 in the section ' The Second Noble Truth'.

2. According to the *Abhidhamma* all sensory impressions are accompanied by pleasant, unpleasant or neutral feelings except the sense of touch. Because the sense of touch is less refined in nature, only pleasant and unpleasant physical sensations are experienced.

3. If we judge or condemn ourselves that some form of desire has arisen, then this judging or condemning can be noted.

4. See chapter 11 for an explanation about effort and concentration.

5. Many practitioners experience fits of laughing during a meditation retreat, as a release of pent-up fear and tension.

6. See chapters 7and 8.

7. I would make an exception if you have stinging pains or burning sensations in your knees. When you experience these kinds of sensations, I would advise you to change posture in order not to (permanently) damage your knees. Furthermore there may be physical limitations making your walking and/or sitting meditation difficult. It is beneficial to discuss this with the teacher and to draw up an appropriate meditation schedule, and, for example, to sit on a chair for the sitting meditation and to use necessary aids, like crutches, during walking meditation.

8. See chapter 13, the fifth purification.

9. See chapters 3, 12 and 14.

PART V

BUDDHISM IN THE WEST

Buddha image in the Thanbodday Paya
(Pagoda of the 500,000 Buddhas), Monywa, Myanmar

Part 5 deals with various subjects that are much discussed in Western society. In all these issues the principles and fruits of the practice of (insight) meditation are applied to daily life in the West, and I will offer some support in relation to these issues.

Chapter 16 deals with illness and health, and in chapter 17 the relationship between meditation and psychotherapy is discussed. In chapter 18 some aspects of sexuality are illuminated, while chapter 19 is devoted to relationships and communication in general. Chapter 20 is devoted to stress, a phenomenon that is much discussed in our society.

HEALTH

1. SOMATIC ILLNESSES

First of all I would like to point to the purely somatic illnesses that can occur, like infections, muscular disorders, (bacterial) infectious diseases or the effects of an accident. These illnesses have an organic or biological cause; they happen to us and initially manifest themselves purely on a physical level.

2. PSYCHIATRIC ILLNESSES

As a second category there are psychiatric illnesses. Examples are schizophrenia, manic depression, psychotic problems and personality disorders. In psychiatric illness there are often deep-seated difficulties at play, possibly caused by traumatic experiences, unfavourable social circumstances, shortcomings in education and upbringing, and sometimes also by hormonal or genetic malfunctioning. There can be difficulties as regards dealing with thoughts and emotions, resulting in behavioural, psychotic or communication problems. This may involve a temporary imbalance, but sometimes these problems are long-term. Traumas, for example, can be so profound that the process of healing takes a very long time. Some disorders may also be so severe that a complete cure is impossible. An example of such an illness is schizophrenia; generally speaking it is only possible to learn to live and cope with the limitations and the vulnerability this disease has caused.

3. PSYCHOSOMATIC PROBLEMS

Psychosomatic problems form the third category: somatic symptoms that have a psychological cause. Deepak Chopra is a medical specialist and one of the best-known modern authors in the field of illness and health. In his book *Creating Health* he enumerates a number of complaints that may be psychosomatic: high blood pressure, heart problems, cancer, chronic fatigue, stomach and intestinal problems, headaches, backache or other physical pains, and respiratory problems like hyperventilation and asthma.

The main cause of psychosomatic problems is stress or psychological tension[1], reducing our immunity, disturbing our energy levels, and as a result all kinds of physical ailments or difficulties can develop. It needs to be pointed out the somatic complaints are not necessarily always due to psychological pressure or problems. A malfunctioning carotid artery may cause headaches, while heart trouble may arise because valves are functioning inadequately. Furthermore, the quality of the food we eat is much more important than was formerly thought.

In previous generations Western doctors paid relatively little attention to possible psychological causes of physical complaints. As a reaction, there was the tendency in the seventies, with the emergence of the 'new age' movement, to 'psychologise' nearly all illnesses. Both approaches can be detrimental. When on the one hand the possible *psychological* aspects are not taken into account, a doctor may not be able to find obvious physical causes of an illness. Often the symptoms are no longer taken seriously, or are allayed by means of painkillers and the like.

When on the other hand the *physical* side is not taken into the equation, the cause of a complaint or an illness is sought in the psyche. In that case the somatic part is not checked properly, while from a bodily point of view there may be all kinds of problems. I have met many people who were the victim of these two limited approaches. It seems most sensible to me that in the case of persistent complaints, both physical and mental causes are investigated. In doing so allopathic, homeopathic, ayurvedic or psychotherapeutic approaches may be used.

The influence of psychological factors on somatic problems is enormous. Results from research carried out by two Americans, Rosenman and Friedman, confirm this. They introduced two styles of behaviour, so-called 'type A-behaviour' and 'type C-behaviour':

- People with 'type A-behaviour' want to do everything quickly, are always in a hurry and easily become impatient. They are very demanding of themselves, ambitious and inclined to interfere when they feel that others are not quick enough. They do more than one thing at the same time, and are in continuous competition with themselves. According to the research, 'type A-behaviour' is caused mainly by upbringing and strong social pressure. This is particularly prevalent in the West and it is (often unconsciously) influencing our behaviour. The research shows that in type A people there is an increased risk of heart infarcts.
- People with 'type C-behaviour' are socially flexible, and they live in a rational, non-emotional manner. Problems are rationalised and often there are blocked emotions. Rosenman and Friedman say that this personality structure is often found in cancer patients.

Over the past few years more and more attention has been given to psychosomatic issues in the literature. Here I would like to restrict myself to just mentioning a few general pointers for managing, diminishing and preventing psychosomatic problems:

- Pay attention to physical problems; don't ignore them.
- Develop an attitude of acceptance concerning stressful emotions and situations.

- Try not to solve all problems alone. Begin (in a safe environment) to talk about emotions or problems. Sharing our suffering can alleviate it, and offers different perspectives in solving problems; it may also deepen our friendships.
- Don't try to do too much; simplify the daily workload.
- Create some inner calm, for example through yoga, tai chi or meditation practice.
- Take time to relax.
- Do something you like (and which is healthy) on a regular basis.
- Take care to get enough physical exercise.
- Dare to say 'no' once in a while when there is too much work to do.

4. '*KILESA* VIRUSES'

Besides the three forms of illness that were described above, there are also certain troublesome emotions that every normal human being knows. These purely psychological moods will perhaps not immediately be experienced and recognised as an illness. However, in Buddhism they *are* seen as pathological, because they lead to pain, sadness, frustration and despair if we don't know how to deal with them wisely, and because they consequently may hinder our mental (and physical) health. They are the so-called *kilesa* or impurities: defilements of the mind, which in Buddhist psychology are said to be the cause of the universal disease of suffering or *dukkha*. Ten *kilesa* are listed (although many more could be mentioned):

1. Greed and attachment (*lobha*)
2. Hatred (*dosa*)
3. Ignorance or lack of a sense of reality (*moha*)

4. Pride and self-righteousness (*māna*)
5. Wrong view or mistaken view of reality (*ditthi*)
6. Sceptical doubt, uncertainty (*vicikicchā*)
7. Dullness, lethargy (*thina*)
8. Restlessness (*uddhacca*)
9. Absence of moral shame (*ahirika*)
10. Absence of moral fear (for criticism) (*anottappa*)

The word *kilesa* comes from Pali and has two meanings: to torture, and to burn. This clearly indicates the unpleasant and unwholesome character of these 'viruses'. When, for example, feelings of hatred are expressed without wisdom, this often has destructive results in relationships and/or in society; when they are suppressed there is an inner fire which may result in feelings of depression or in psychosomatic problems. Or in the case of desire: when desires cannot be fulfilled, there is an inner burning or torturing, and this creates feelings of frustration. When desires do get fulfilled this can lead to addiction and consequently to all kinds of other mental, physical or social problems. This is why the *kilesa* – which we know in many guises – are viewed as unwholesome, pathogenic or poisonous. They result in various forms of imbalance and illness, both in body and mind.

THE ROLE OF MEDITATION

There are various ways in which meditation can play a role in illness. Where it concerns problems, diseases or handicaps that are incurable, or that can rarely be cured, meditation can help us to accept the illness and the resulting limitations. This may encourage and reinforce finding a new equilibrium. An elementary tool in this is *karunā* or compassion. The cultivation and practice of compassion is extremely important and adds a deeper value and richness to life. Compassion is seen in Buddhist psychology as one of the four *brahmavihāra* or sublime states of mind; the others are lovingkindness, sympathetic joy and equanimity.[2]

Cultivating compassion for our own suffering and that of others is essential for healing and for a bearable existence as human beings. Compassion works like a source of heat in a damp, cold and uninhabitable place. It opens up avenues to gentleness, enabling us to cope with pain and misery in a warm and accepting way. Through meditation a kind and healing openness towards pain and difficulties can be developed. In Buddhism the practice of meditation is viewed as the most effective remedy against the many *kilesa* viruses of desire, hatred and ignorance, and the psychosomatic illnesses they cause. We could see it as a detoxification programme which anybody – Buddhist or non-Buddhist – can follow, with the aim of becoming more liberated or healed from the *kilesa* viruses, as well as from the physical disharmony they cause.

In the practice of *samatha* or tranquillity meditation[3] the emphasis is placed on developing concentration, or one-pointedness of the mind, by suppressing mental hindrances. This works as a process of substitution. For instance *mettā-bhāvanā* or meditation on lovingkindness gradually softens and lessens the tendency to feel hatred and impatience. This acts as a slow-working palliative without harmful side effects.

With *vipassanā* or insight meditation[4] we develop mindfulness of mental and physical phenomena, without judging or condemning whatever is being observed, and without clinging to whatever arises in the field of consciousness. For that moment, we do not (or no longer) identify with the object of mindfulness, because we are observing it without preference, just naming or noting it. This creates a subtle distance in relation to the physical or mental pain, and takes the suffering out of the pain. The mental impurities or defilements listed above can lose their controlling power and eventually be uprooted or eradicated completely. By practising *vipassanā* or insight meditation it is possible that ultimately all pathogenic *kilesa* are rendered completely harmless.

Vipassanā meditation could therefore be called a 'painkiller' and the Buddha can be seen as a physician who discovered a remedy for the universal disease of *dukkha* or suffering. This medicine is a spiritual therapy or detoxification programme that leads to a more skilful handling, to prevention and ultimately to a definitive ending of the *kilesa* viruses.

This clearly shows the practical aspect of Buddhism, which in this respect is mainly a way of life, offering a path that can be walked by anyone who is open to it.

In general most people judge illness and everything that feels unpleasant as something negative; this negative judgement often causes additional problems. Illness can also be seen as the result or *vipāka* of karmic impurities or tensions that were stored in body and/or mind, and that now come to the surface. In this way illness can be considered a spiritual gift, offering the possibility to work through it *now*, and to let go of the karmic burden.

Illness can be viewed as a welcome healing process, and many meditators have the experience that, if in times of sickness care and attention is given to the observation of whatever is happening, the fever or illness clears up a lot quicker. If it concerns an incurable pain or disease, mindfulness can probably not guarantee a cure, but proves to be of great value as a way to process the grief or the sorrow arising from having such a condition or handicap. This happens because we no longer identify with the condition we find ourselves in. It supports liberation from the processes of fighting, mourning or being a victim, and helps to integrate the handicap into our lives.

In this respect the work of Jon Kabat-Zinn is fascinating. This American doctor found that some patients suffered from chronic pain: headaches, backaches after a back injury, vague psychosomatic pains and so on. The medical staff at the hospital in Massachusetts where he worked did not know what to do with these people, and they were usually – after extensive check ups – just prescribed some painkillers, which did not have any effect either. Over the years Kabat-Zinn developed a very successful course in pain management, which consists of mindfulness exercises in combination with yoga.

Sickness is often viewed as something negative. But it can also point to an understanding that there is more to life than just prosperity, youthful power and beauty. In Buddhist psychology illness is described as *samvega-vatthu*: an experience that calls for spiritual urgency. The Spanish theologian, author and mystic Raimon Panikkar calls this a breaking point in life. We can get overwhelmed by suffering, or wallow in it. However, it can also offer us the opportunity to reconsider, and to begin a new, purified life. Many people experience a spiritual awakening during their illness or as a result of it, and they begin to look for deeper values in life. In this way illness may become a source of insight and compassion.

NOTES

1. See chapter 20 for a more elaborate explanation of the term 'stress'.
2. For more details about the four divine states of consciousness see chapter 7.
3. See chapter 8 for a detailed explanation about tranquillity meditation.
4. See chapters 9 and 10.

17

MEDITHERAPY

For various reasons emotions, problems or inner conflicts can become quite difficult to handle. Therefore many people in the West seek help from a counsellor, psychologist, psychiatrist or social worker. One person may carry a heavier negative or neurotic burden in their lives than another. But the large number of people seeking help from a therapist shows that many people have psychiatric problems to such an extent that they feel the need to enter one form of therapy or another.

So what exactly is therapy? Perhaps the best way of describing it is as a process of curing and healing. The diseases or scars in this context are usually unconscious and unresolved issues, problems and emotions causing the body and/or the mind to contract. There are many kinds of therapies, like Gestalt, bioenergetics, Reichian therapy, Transactional Analysis and psychosynthesis. Most of these therapies focus on making the client aware of suppressed and unresolved issues and emotions, and on learning how to express them, without causing harm, in order to get free from them. Many therapies also give positive new input as wholesome seeds for the future.

Buddhist psychology states that there are eight causes for difficulties and psychological knots which in extreme cases may result in *ummattaka*, a state of – hopefully – temporary mental derangement, despair, insanity or impulsive behaviour, causing people to consciously or unconsciously inflict pain and grief on themselves or others. In the Buddhist texts the following eight causes are mentioned:

1. Inadequate dealing with sensual and sexual desire.
2. Inadequate coping with anger or hatred.
3. Conscious or unconscious clinging to a clouded or distorted view of reality.
4. Ignorance, not seeing the consequences of one's actions.
5. Being negatively influenced and carried away by other people's ideas.
6. Organic disorders as can be seen in people who suffer from non-congenital brain damage, a brain tumour or forms of schizophrenia. Hormonal disorders are also in this category: they can cause people to be thrown off balance.
7. Abuse or misuse of intoxicants such as alcohol, drugs or medication.
8. Devastating or traumatic loss or misfortune. In this context the following kinds of loss are mentioned: loss – unexpected or otherwise – of relatives and friends, property, health, physical capabilities, a good name and reputation, and finally loss of a healthy sense of discrimination between what is wholesome and skilful and what is not.

Obvious examples of *ummattaka* are intimidation or rape caused by suppressed sexual desire; the madness of war caused by hatred; racial discrimination caused by a deluded and mistaken view of reality; unintended conflicts, stupidities or traffic accidents caused by excessive alcohol intake, and suicidal behaviour caused by devastating loss.

Less severe forms of the aforementioned eight factors, particularly if they are not dealt with skilfully, may also result in visible or invisible pain and suffering. It is quite an art to live harmoniously and not become the victim of these emotions and situations.

THERAPEUTIC ASPECTS OF MINDFULNESS

The Buddha, too, in his efforts to gain enlightenment, was searching for a solution to human pain and grief. Eventually he found a
simple but at the same time radical therapy or healing method to
understand and end our suffering caused by desire, attachment,
hatred and delusion.

Most forms of psychotherapy work with specific mental knots
and contractions. They offer the client a way to become aware of
unskilful and unwholesome conditionings and to cope with unresolved grieving in a skilful manner, enabling him or her to learn
to accept the loss and to relate more wisely with unwholesome
tendencies in themselves.

Developing mindfulness through the practice of *vipassanā* or
insight meditation can be of enormous benefit to this healing process. But mindfulness is not just a way to deal skilfully with existing problems and to realise therapeutic insight; it also prevents
difficulties from arising by developing awareness of ordinary, not
immediately problematic emotions, thoughts and other experiences. If we use such everyday experiences as objects of meditation future difficulties can be prevented. This preventative power
is strengthened by deeper intuitive and existential insight, which
then acts as a guide, leading us beyond our ordinary conditioned
limitations.

Some years ago the term 'transpersonal' was coined in America
to describe forms of therapy and psychology that transcend the
boundaries of the ego and gradually shift from psychotherapy to
spiritual awakening. I would call *vipassanā* meditation a radical
transpersonal life therapy, because all human experience is used as
an object of awareness. Through the practice of insight meditation eventually all worldly experience is transcended[1], which can
be realised through careful and close observation or awareness,
from moment to moment, of whatever arises in body and mind.
We simply observe what is predominant in any given moment,

without doing anything with or about it, just letting it be. We are not pushing it away and not trying to grasp or hold on to it, only observing it as it is, without trying to change it in any way.

Whatever we observe we name or note: hearing as 'hearing', seeing as 'seeing', thinking as 'thinking', feeling as 'feeling', emotions as 'emotion' and so on. An obvious difference with most forms of psychotherapy is that in *vipassanā* meditation we do not need to go into the content of the emotions or thoughts. It is enough just to observe and note them as they are, without doing anything. So there is no analysing, reflecting or judging, because this would mean that the observation and awareness is no longer direct. However, if we notice that we are analysing or judging, then we can note 'analysing' or 'judging' again. In this way we develop intuitive insight into the phenomenon of thinking, feeling or experiencing an emotion. It does not matter what kind of object it is that we observe. Whether it is pleasant or unpleasant, skilful or unskilful, thinking, hearing, seeing or feeling . . . in meditation practice it makes no difference. The only thing we need to do is to observe what is predominant here and now. It does not matter what it is; all the physical and mental experiences or phenomena are of equal value.[2]

NON-IDENTIFICATION

Noting or naming makes the observation transpersonal: we no longer identify with the thought or the emotion. It is no longer *our* sadness, anger or thought, but a feeling or thought process which is observed and noted objectively. Roberto Assagioli, the founder of psychosynthesis, used the term 'disidentification' in this context. He referred to a subtle inner disconnection from the 'self': body, feelings, thoughts and their contents, emotions and other experiences are not seen as personal or as 'mine', but are observed as objectively perceived phenomena. This results in the experience of a subtle inner freedom, because the burden of the idea that something is ours has fallen away. Matthew Flickstein, a psychotherapist and meditation teacher in the U.S. offers a valuable addition to this in his book *Swallowing the River Ganges*. He distinguishes between a detached and a non-attached perspective. Detachment, the opposite of attachment, can easily create an attitude of pushing away or rejection of what is being observed. Non-attachment – he states – has a more equanimous quality. It is being present without attempting to cling or resist an experience.

In the same way I would say that the term non-identification is more precise and less confusing than the term disidentification. When there is non-identification, spaciousness arises where thoughts and emotions are treated as temporarily perceived or observed guests. In a very simple way this mechanism can be experienced in those moments when we are talking to a good friend, counsellor or therapist about something that leaves us stuck. We put our problem on the table as it were, often enabling us to become aware of what exactly is the matter from a healthy distance. No reaction from the listener is required.

Inner observation and naming or noting of what is happening here and now works in the same way. Contact with a therapist or with a therapy group can be a good foundation and support for loosening the contraction around deep-rooted problems and wounds, and for learning how to resolve them, making it easier to observe them from a place of openness and spaciousness. But it is not always necessary to enter therapy: some people carry more neurotic baggage than others.

In any case, the process of non-identification obviously acts as a valuable friend and guide. It can be used not only in times of distress, but also as a preventative measure and as the guardian of a healthy inner balance in general. And ultimately it will enable us to be completely purified of unwholesome forces in the mind. This is the power of 'meditherapy'.

NOTES

1. See chapter 14.
2. See chapter 10 for more information on the practice of insight meditation.

18

SEXUAL DESIRE

Sexual desire and the urge to procreate are two of the strongest driving forces in nature. For many people sexual desire also proves to be a troublesome force. Just look at the blockages, frustrations, obsessions and taboos in this area. This chapter is an attempt to reflect on how (Theravāda) Buddhism views the experience and handling of sexual desire.

Firstly let us look the Buddha's own sexual life. Even though it is never mentioned in the traditional scriptures, as a prince living in a palace, the Buddha may quite possibly have had a harem, which in those days was the norm for people in high places. Women probably danced for him, gave him exotic fruit to eat, made sensuous music, and offered him all kinds of pleasures. At a young age he married a beautiful woman, and together they must have had a fulfilling life.

As mentioned in chapter 1, at a certain moment the prince woke up from this pleasurable dream and began to discover different, less pleasant aspects of life. He decided to renounce his 'princely' life at the palace; living in seclusion he started to look for deeper wisdom. In an extreme manner he tried – perhaps as a reaction to his earlier life as a prince – to fight all desires and sensual passions. After seven years of ascetic practice and self-mortification, he realised that suppressing and rejecting human needs, just like his former way of life, did not result in the desired insights either. Eventually the young seeker found a middle way,[1] discovering the truth he was looking for, and he was given the title of Buddha, 'he who has awakened from ignorance'.

He realised this wisdom through merely observing, attentively being aware of all phenomena in body and mind, without chasing after them or suppressing them, without judging and condemning whatever arose in him. He applied this to all possible human experiences, and must have done so too with erotic feelings and sexual desire when Māra tried to seduce him.[2]

When the Buddha, after attaining enlightenment, started to share his insights with others, he always made a distinction as regards the practice of his teachings between monastics and lay people. In his eyes living a celibate life as a monk or nun was the most appropriate way to practise the Dhamma. Nuns and monks do not need to earn their own livelihood, but can live on the basis of the generosity of lay people. Furthermore, monks and nuns do not spend time in a sexual relationship and they are free from social duties as husband, wife, father or mother. This gives them more time for the practice of meditation, for study and for sharing their insights with others.

In time the Buddha set out all kinds of guidelines for the protection of the monastic community; these could be called preventative measures so as not to stray from the monastic path. The Buddha concluded that sexual desire intoxicates the mind and prevents clarity. Besides, it can easily lead to a sexual relationship and – certainly in an era when contraceptives were not known – to having children with all the obligations and responsibilities that entails. Therefore the Buddha stipulated that sexual contact is not part of monastic life. Mentally or emotionally monks or nuns do not need to stop sexual thoughts or feelings, but they should not act on these. Just as with any other physical and mental phenomena, there is the attempt to merely observe sexual feelings and to note them, as they are and as long as they are clearly there, without having to do anything with or about them. In the psychology of meditation sexual desire does not need to be judged (as good or bad). Neither does it need to be curtailed or stimulated, but it can simply be integrated as a meditation object, treating it as one of many human experiences in a friendly and accepting way. It is just as valuable as a sound, the rising and falling of the abdomen, a thought or a pleasant or unpleasant sensation.

In practice however, it often proves difficult to keep observing erotic feelings in an open but also consistent way, without unknowingly suppressing these feelings, or being seduced by their power. The Buddha indicated very clearly that a monk or a nun always had the freedom to disrobe and leave the order, without this being seen as shameful or as a defeat. Ordaining as a monk or a nun in Buddhism is not considered a vocation for the rest of our life, but as a special training for the cultivation of mindfulness, insight and inner freedom, that we can follow for as long (or as short) a time as we wish. When we no longer want to do this, or are no longer able to, we are at liberty to disrobe. It is good to realise that the Buddha did not see celibacy as the ultimate goal, but more as an additional training where we develop insight and learn to deal skilfully with life (and therefore also with sexual desire). For those who are ready for this, it can be very beneficial to ordain as a monk or a nun for a longer or shorter period.

A lay person can practise the Dhamma in a less intensive manner. Lay practitioners don't need to live a celibate life, and they have the freedom to engage in a sexual relationship and to get married and have children. This results in more social obligations, and so lay people can experience in a different way that sexual desire can cause a lot of hurt when it is not handled skilfully. We all know how unrequited love is very painful. Falling in love with another man or woman who is already part of an existing relationship, and adultery are often a source of pain and confusion. Because as lay people we live busier lives, it is probably even more difficult to be able to observe desires meditatively. Nevertheless the texts mention many stories of lay people with an active sexual life who did realise a degree of enlightenment. Not leading a life of celibacy apparently does not necessarily mean that it obstructs or disturbs the spiritual path. According to Buddhist psychology sexual urges are completely extinguished only when someone has realised the third stage of enlightenment.[3]

For Western people in particular, who often have a negative self-image and are judgemental with regard to the experience of sexuality, living a monastic life long-term is in my view not advisable in many cases. It can easily become an escape, and result in a (perhaps even stronger) strategy of suppression, instead of a training that leads to insight. It can be very refreshing and important for many people to investigate their sexuality and not turn away from it.

During a chosen period of intensive practice it is always advised to observe celibacy. This has the advantage of a cool and clear mind that can observe continuously for longer periods of time, without following or repressing desires, resistance and other emotions. So when we are practising meditation, we really are part-time monks or nuns; and this is certainly recommended when looking for insight and seeking inner freedom from painful passions. Whether in daily life we choose a sexual relationship or not does not really matter. With the help of insight meditation we can learn to relate to sexual desire and other experiences in ourselves in an open and friendly way, regardless of how we live our lives.

NOTES

1. A middle way between indulging in pleasure and self-mortification.
2. See chapter 15.
3. See chapter 14 for an explanation of the different stages of enlightenment.

19

RELATIONSHIPS AND COMMUNICATION

Perhaps one of the most profound and intimate experiences we know as human beings is a love-relationship. This chapter is an attempt to look at this phenomenon from a spiritual perspective.

Most of us experience, at one time or another in our lives, a love-relationship in some form. This can bring all kinds of things in its wake. In the first place there is being in love. We feel as though we are in the seventh heaven, and we experience everything as beautiful; we lose our head, do crazy things and there often is sexual pleasure as well. In the next phase the sense of being in love changes somewhat. We are confronted again with the ordinary demands of everyday life. Now we also begin to see each other's darker sides. With dark side I mean the unpleasant, unconscious limitations, blockages and conditionings we carry around with us. When the relationship becomes less exciting, 'more normal', they manifest in the form of strong feelings of dependency, fear of commitment or intimacy, grumbling, complaining, not being able to accept criticism, nagging, self-righteousness, feelings of inferiority or superiority. All of us, with the exception of *arahats* (fully enlightened people), have our tendencies and difficult conditionings, quite often causing us to react or respond in unwise ways that destroy any connection we might have felt.

Many people stop the relationship at this stage. The partner does not live up to the ideal image, the conditionings and resulting pain are too strong. Sometimes the relationship is drawn out in a destructive and tortuous manner, but often from that time onwards it becomes a relationship based on habit, without any real intimacy. Sometimes things do work out well. In that case, apart from economical (survival) motives – which in the West often are the basis of a relationship – both partners may realise fulfilment of physical, intellectual, emotional and spiritual needs, and the relationship is seen as a valuable learning process.

Becoming aware of emotions and thought patterns plays an important, healing role. Problems and misunderstandings mostly arise from illusions that we unknowingly cherish. In Buddhist psychology four possible forms of illusion or *vipallāsa* are mentioned:

1. That which is impermanent is (mistakenly) seen as permanent.
2. That which is impure (and creating suffering) is seen as pure.
3. That which is in essence 'not beautiful' is seen as 'beautiful'. It needs to be pointed out that 'not beautiful' does not always mean ugly. According to Buddhist psychology it is just an opinion to think that something beautiful or ugly. Ultimately there is no such judgement attached to experience.
4. That which is in essence selfless is interpreted as 'self' or as 'mine'.

Generally speaking, these illusions manifest at first only in perception. Later they establish themselves in thought, and finally they become incorporated into convictions and ideas we have about ourselves, about others and the world at large. In most love-relationships these illusions clearly come to the surface, but mostly without us recognising them. Just think of the period when we have fallen in love. We meet somebody, who stimulates us one way or another, and we think everything about this man or woman is great. Beautiful to look at, a wonderful voice, kind, attentive to what we do or say, and before we know it we have fallen into the trap. In fact, he or she is not beautiful but we make this up. We just interpret things through the rose-tinted glasses of hallucination number three. In any case, being in love goes together with the second illusion, namely that the imperfect, conditioned other is pure or perfect. We attribute all kinds of lofty qualities to the other and to the relationship we build. These thoughts reinforce the illusion; we feel so intensely happy that it seems divine and everlasting (illusion number one).

Intimacy deepens, not only in relation to our feelings and thoughts, but our ideas begin to change as well. We make plans to start living together and building a life or a family together. The next step is that we begin to identify with the partner and unconsciously start to own him or her as 'mine'. We take more and more aspects of the other into consideration and people around us begin to see us more as a 'couple'. This pattern can sometimes be so powerful and suffocating that we can hardly live or be happy without the other, as is the case in symbiotic relationships.

This picture is of course in sharp contrast with romantic love-dramas where love is praised as being perfect happiness. From a Buddhist perspective love is – as long as it is based on one or more forms of illusion – not lofty at all. Mostly it is based on unconscious, and therefore enslaving patterns, like sensual pleasure, attachment, fear (to be alone or to lose), and a deeply rooted misunderstanding as regards reality, which in turn makes us deluded over and over again. This is why in nearly every spiritual tradition there is the opportunity to lead a monastic life, where conditioned love and illusions have fewer sources of nourishment. In that case we don't need to expend energy into something that is saturated with impurity.

RELATIONSHIP AS A SOURCE OF INSIGHT

Above I have outlined one part of the story, when relationships are fed by (unconsciously cherished) illusions, which result in pain and sorrow. Yet a relationship can also be a source of rest. Fulfilling our basic human needs gives a sense of calm, because – whether it is conditioned or not – loving physical contact, being able to share pain and pleasure intimately, and the knowledge that someone cares a lot about us, are what most people need to live harmoniously. There are plenty of examples of people who flourished because of an intimate love relationship.

Furthermore, a relationship can also become a source of insight when we begin to view it as a practical training ground for awakening. Whether we want to or not, after the initial falling in love we will be confronted with ourselves in various ways, perhaps even more than when we live a 'simple' life as a single person. An intimate partner can function as a mirror, not only for our pleasant characteristics, but also for our normally invisible dark sides. Sometimes this can be very painful and challenging. In most relationships that break up, this confrontational aspect is not or cannot be handled skilfully. Disappointments and expectations that are based on illusions are projected onto the other person in the guise of accusations and resentment.

Becoming aware can have a clarifying function in this. We learn to recognise (underlying) thoughts and emotions in ourselves, when previously we projected them onto the other, because we were not aware of them. An intimate partner can be seen as a fusspot who always has something to complain or grumble about; we can also see him or her as a sounding board or mirror that from time to time shows us our own blind spots. And the relationship can function as a way to learn how to deal with emotions skilfully. If there is trust, we can be vulnerable and find out how we can be spacious with fear, anger or sexual desire in a wise manner, without demeaning ourselves, and not harming the other person either. This can be an informative and patient training process, where mindfulness is a healing force that creates a wholesome and open relationship.

I noticed that amongst those who practise and teach *vipassanā* meditation, little attention is paid to communication. The Buddha gave a number of guidelines in this area.[1] A few times I experimented – with experienced meditators – with an exercise called 'attention in contact' at the end of a retreat or during days of meditation. I asked the participants to sit opposite one another and to follow the instructions given below.

EXERCISE: ATTENTION IN CONTACT

Sit in a comfortable manner with your eyes closed and meditate. After a few minutes open your eyes and look at the person sitting opposite you. Observe and note what is presenting itself moment by moment in or to you: opening the eyes, looking or seeing, thoughts, physical or emotional feelings, and so on, without doing anything with what you encounter. Greet one another after a few minutes, and again note what is predominant: the intention to greet, the sound of the voice, smiling . . . Then in turn say something about yourself. Something that preoccupies you, something you like, have discovered, find difficult or have experienced . . . something that arises in you in that moment. Both of you observe and note again from moment to moment what is recognised: the intention to speak, speaking or listening, looking at the other, thoughts, physical or emotional reactions. Keep this mindful conversation going for a couple of minutes; when you want to say something specific do this, say goodbye and continue to meditate with your eyes closed.

What turned out to be so special about this exercise was that the participants could learn in a simple way to stay present with themselves in the contact with others, and could recognise things in themselves that normally they were not aware of. Because of the complexity of communication and the patterns we can notice in ourselves, we should probably have some meditation experience before doing this exercise. It needs also be pointed out beforehand that the exercise is totally voluntary. Particularly at the end of a longer meditation retreat this exercise can simplify the transition from the silence to our busy 'everyday' lives.[2]

Through greater self-knowledge, we will be ruled less by our darker sides in our contacts with others. That is why the Buddha gave his last encouragement before he died: *Be an island unto yourself.* He did not mean that we should go and live on an uninhabited island, and live our lives in isolation from the rest of the world. He meant a kind of basic stability and security; not drowning in sensual desires, the urge to be, ideas or judgements and unawareness. Such a stability can be developed by means of mindfulness practice: on the meditation cushion or meditation seat at home, at work, in our relationships, in contact with others, and – when we feel the need – in intensive retreats, as a source of nourishment for greater self-insight. We can learn in this way to look through our illusions and projections, and to get more in touch with the reality of the here and now.

With this attitude it is easier to enter into a commitment with a partner, a monastic community, a job, children and so on. These commitments can be seen as valuable tools for growing and learning, from which we may draw much happiness and joy, while at the same time not expecting that they automatically guarantee an everlasting, perfect happiness. However, these relationships can become a solid ground for developing mindfulness, so as not to drown in the stream of illusions and projections. The Buddha ended his last advice with the words: *Be heedful, be mindful in the here and now.* In this way we cultivate freedom in commitment.

NOTES

1. See for example right speech, the third aspect of the Eightfold Path, in chapter 3.

2. During intensive retreats meditators can use the interviews with the meditation teachers as an awareness exercise as well. Entering and leaving, looking, registering intentions to say something, speaking, listening, thoughts, emotions are all phenomena that can be noticed. Sharing after a weekly meditation session can likewise give an extra dimension. In this way, conversations that are normally carried out unconsciously or in a half-conscious manner, can become a field of mindfulness and a source of insight.

20

STRESS MANAGEMENT

Nowadays the word 'stress' is a very common term, and nearly every week it is mentioned in the media. Stress is something all of us (may) encounter everywhere. So what exactly is stress? The word probably derives from the Latin *stringere*, which means 'pulling tight' or 'to apply tension'. The Austrian scientist Hans Selye introduced the term 'stress' into biological and medical science, and he described it as 'pressure' or 'tension'. In everyday usage it has a very broad meaning, indicating all kinds of tensions, both in our private lives as well as in the work place.

Stress can be defined as 'a state where there is a disturbance of the equilibrium between the demands that are placed on us and the possibilities that we have to fulfil those demands.' This definition implies that stress is subjective. What by one person is experienced as stress, does not necessarily mean the same for another. It is also very important how we deal with the burden that is experienced. And stress need not always be a result of overload, but can be caused by too little stimulation as well, which results in boredom and displeasure.

In the literature about stress, different aspects are mentioned with regard to the experience of stress.

SOURCES OF STRESS (STRESSORS)

Two types can be distinguished: external and inner sources of stress. By external sources of stress we mean situations and events that happen to us, whether we want to or not. We cannot do anything about them; they are outside our immediate control. These sources of stress can be subdivided into four categories (from light to heavy):

1. Everyday events, which cause discomfort and tension, like a train that is delayed, car or computer breakdown, or forgetting something important.
2. Chronic burdening circumstances causing stress by their lasting, 'dragging' nature. Examples of this are long-term illness, chronic lack of sleep (caused, for instance, by a baby who cries during the night), or relationship issues.
3. Far-reaching changes or events in our lives. Examples of this category are the passing away of a partner or family member, divorce or the break-up of a long-term relationship, dismissal or the news that we suffer from a serious or incurable illness.
4. Traumatic events. The word 'trauma' comes from Greek and means 'wound'. Traumatic experiences are those events that are so intrusive and shocking that they leave a big physical and/or psychological wound. Sometimes such experiences are expected, but often they happen unexpectedly, and in any case there are intense feelings of stress and powerlessness. Examples are a serious car accident, rape, natural catastrophes or war.

The extent of stress that is the result of these circumstances and events is not the same for everyone. What is a shocking or traumatic situation for one person may not be so for another. Furthermore it turns out that in particular the accumulation of events can lead to great pressure, because in that situation there is too little time for recovery from the event in question. Our flexibility and strength are no longer adequate to meet the blow in a subsequent situation of stress.

Inner sources of stress are related to our personalities and conditionings. Examples of these are:

- The urge to be perfect
- A great sense of responsibility
- Sensitivity to authority
- Being introverted in character
- Living with an attitude of 'I run therefore I am', or 'I help therefore I am'
- The tendency to prove ourselves in order to give ourselves a sense of self-worth
- Fear of criticism or failure
- Insecurity

These conditionings arise from our upbringing, from (conclusions drawn from) life experiences or – if we believe in these – perhaps from previous lives. Most people have some characteristics that may cause stress.

PHYSICAL REACTION TO STRESSORS

When a stressor presents itself a physiological reaction is caused, called stress reaction or 'fight-or-flight syndrome'. This is described as a natural, co-ordinated chemical mobilisation of the entire body in a threatening situation (physical or psychological). At this stage the so-called stress hormones like adrenaline and cortisol are released and absorbed into the bloodstream. This state of high alertness usually is accompanied by a number of physiological phenomena, like sharpening of the visual and auditory faculties, deeper and quicker breathing, higher blood pressure, tensing of the muscles, or sweating hands. In short: we are alert and on our guard!

THE COGNITIVE IMPLICATIONS

This state of alarm determines the cognitive meaning or interpretation we give to the situation, and in turn the interpretation we have of a situation can reinforce or weaken the physical reaction. An example of a reinforcing interpretation is the thought that we are obliged to do something, that we are responsible for the problem. A stress-reducing interpretation can be a thought that puts the situation into perspective, or a sense of humour.

EMOTIONAL REACTIONS

Emotions like fear, sadness, powerlessness, anger or a sense of guilt arise due to the interaction between the physical stress reaction and the interpretation. Such emotions are a natural and human reaction to the aforementioned stimuli.

BEHAVIOURAL REACTIONS OR COPING

The way we handle all these aspects of stress is called 'coping' or stress management. Coping can be described as the process we are using to face sources of stress we consider burdening, as well as the emotions these stressors evoke. Coping can be both adequate and inadequate.

Inadequate coping is, generally speaking, related to the fact that we do not, or do not sufficiently, recognise emotions; this is accompanied by stress symptoms and results in inadequate behaviour: complaining, aggressive, uncoordinated or evasive behaviour, excessive eating, smoking or drinking. In turn, inadequate behaviour can lead to long-term traumatic stress reactions, psychosomatic problems, or symptoms of being overworked or burnout[1] symptoms.

Adequate coping does not lead to unhealthy reactions; there is a skilful cognitive, emotional and behavioural handling of stress or stressors.

MEDITATION AS STRESS MANAGEMENT

Awareness in relation to these aspects of stress can be seen as an important condition and foundation for adequately coping with stress. Meditation proves to be a very suitable 'tool' to realise this. Many people who in one way or another are under a lot of psychological pressure, are overworked or have symptoms of burnout, become interested in meditation, and I think meditation practice can offer a lot. The effect of meditation as stress management depends on the type of meditation that is practised. In Buddhism two forms of meditation are distinguished: tranquillity or relaxation meditation, and insight or mindfulness meditation.[2]

In *samatha* or tranquillity meditation the emphasis is on cultivating calm, rest and relaxation by directing our attention to one point. The concentration we develop in this way is very beneficial and refreshing, and goes deeper and deeper as we continue. This can create an oasis of tranquillity in a busy and stressful life. We might call it a healthy palliative or tension-reducing method of stress management.

In *vipassanā* or insight meditation relaxation is also achieved, but this is not the main goal. Developing mindfulness is at the heart of this second form of meditation. It is a process of becoming aware that leads to the realisation of clarity of mind, inner freedom and (the happiness of) insight.

For many people practising this second type of meditation is more difficult than the first one, because sometimes we are confronted directly with our blind spots, unresolved emotions or mechanisms that cause stress. At the same time insight meditation can be very valuable and applicable, however. It gives insight into our own functioning, in how and when stress arises, and how we (can) cognitively and emotionally deal with it.

BENEFICIAL EFFECTS OF INSIGHT MEDITATION

I have seen the following beneficial effects from the practice of insight meditation:

- We become more and more quickly aware of our needs. We also become more aware of signals (tiredness or tension), and we can (learn to) listen to these.
- Through greater acceptance of thoughts and emotions there is a relaxation in the here and now.
- Becoming aware of and naming or noting what is happening at the moment in body and mind, leads to non-identification in relation to what is being observed. As a natural result of this the mental or physical phenomenon that we previously were not aware of, becomes objectified in that moment. We no longer react unconsciously to the experience, and further conditioning and stress reactions are considerably reduced. This objectification has a very sobering and healing effect. I think of problems that can arise through identification and 'counter-projection'[3] in the relationship with clients, or with our job and responsibilities in general. Objectifying means that we see things from a matter-of-fact, down-to-earth perspective.
- Right there, at the moment of awareness, we are offered a choice. We can accept the experience, look at it in a level-headed and rational way, leave it for what it is for a while, or do something that is relaxing, whatever we think is needed to handle the situation skilfully.
- Acknowledging or recognising and naming (unresolved) emotions and experiences has a liberating effect. Subcon-

scious and often unhealthy 'fumes' are allowed to come to the surface and to dissolve. Mindfulness and awareness can also bring defence mechanisms or persistent thought patterns to light. By becoming aware of them we slowly experience inner spaciousness, and we are able to deal with what is happening in the moment with more openness and freedom. This inner space can also be experienced in managing psychosomatic problems. In some cases these become less overpowering or can even disappear completely. And if such problems are long-term or incurable, at least we are less at the mercy of pain and illness.

- Awareness is stress reducing and preventative. For example, we realise more easily that we are rushing, on our toes, overtired or crossing boundaries, and that we keep working at all cost. In this way awareness can have a positive influence in the prevention of or timely intervention as regards burnout symptoms.

- Finally insight meditation can, according to Buddhist psychology, lead to deeper levels of insight and transformation of consciousness, as described in chapters 12, 13 and 14.

In short, meditation can offer much in the field of stress management. Relaxation meditation is calming and palliative or stress reducing in nature. In insight meditation awareness is the key element. It is fascinating and inspiring to see how particularly in the health care sector and in the service sector, there is a growing interest in mindfulness training.

In the psychiatric hospital in the Netherlands where I work, in 1997 we started a programme called 'Methods of Stress Management' for the more than 2,400 people working in this hospital in one capacity or another. In this hospital there have recently been mergers and a lot of reorganisation, and many new developments in relation to the care provided, the groups of clients/patients, and job delineation. These developments are often necessary, but at the same time give rise to insecurity and uncertainty. Interviews I did with the nursing staff showed that many of them noticed symptoms of stress in themselves or in others.[4]

In order to support colleagues in their individual stress management the ward where I work has created a programme of refresher courses and post-diploma training, offering various stress management techniques that are not yet well known in the Netherlands. The overwhelming interest and positive reactions surprised us. In preliminary feedback, the participants of the course 'Insight Meditation as Stress Management' indicated that the training contributed to greater awareness of the determining factors in the building up of stress, and of the manner of dealing with stress. They also stated that they could directly apply to their daily lives what they had learned in the workshops.

It often strikes me how surprised people are about the simplicity, immediate applicability and the natural healing power of mindfulness. I suspect that in the future the practice of insight meditation will become more and more integrated into Western society, not only as a spiritual path, but also as a supporting tool in the prevention of and coping with stress.

NOTES

1. 'Burnout' can be described as an emotional state of depletion or exhaustion that arises particularly in professions that involve working with people. This state is often accompanied by a distant, indifferent or negative attitude to the clients, and with a reduced sense of competence.

2. See chapters 8, 9 and 10 for details about these forms of practice.

3. 'Counter-projection' is a term used in the health care system, generally referring to a considerable emotional involvement of carers with their clients.

4. Tiredness, repeatedly complaining, and psychosomatic problems scored very highly; furthermore it became evident that on many wards there was a lot of absenteeism due to illness.

APPENDICES

Wat Xieng Thong, Luang Prabang, Laos

APPENDIX I

THE FOUR FOUNDATIONS OF MINDFULNESS

Translation (from the Pali) of the *Satipatthāna Sutta*, The Discourse on the Foundations of Mindfulness. This discourse can be found in the *Majjhima Nikāya* (see Recommended Reading, appendix 5).

1. Thus I have heard. At one time, the Blessed One was staying among the Kurus, in a market town of theirs called Kammāsadhamma. There he addressed the monks thus: 'Bhikkhus',[1] and the monks replied: 'Venerable Sir'. And the Blessed One spoke as follows:

2. 'Bhikkhus, this path, namely the four foundations of mindfulness, is the direct path for the purification of beings, for the overcoming of sorrow and distress, for the disappearance of pain and sadness, for reaching the right path, for the realisation of *nibbāna*.

3. 'What are the four foundations? In this teaching a bhikkhu abides contemplating the body as body[2], ardent, fully aware and mindful, having put aside hankering and fretting for the world. He abides contemplating feelings as feelings, ardent, fully aware and mindful, having put aside hankering and fretting for the world. He abides contemplating mind as mind, ardent, fully aware and mindful, having put aside hankering and fretting for the world. He abides contemplating *dhammas* as *dhammas*,[3] ardent,

fully aware and mindful, having put aside hankering and fretting for the world.'

MINDFULNESS OF THE BODY
(*kāyānupassanā*)

I. *Mindfulness of Breathing*

4. 'And how, bhikkhus, does a bhikkhu abide contemplating the body as body? In this teaching a monk, having gone to the forest, or to the root of a tree, or to an empty hut, sits down cross-legged, holding his body erect, establishing his mindfulness on the breathing. Mindfully he breathes in, mindfully he breathes out.[4] Breathing in a long breath, he knows "I breathe in long", and breathing out a long breath, he knows "I breathe out long". Breathing in a short breath, he knows "I breathe in short", and breathing out a short breath, he knows "I breathe out short". He trains himself thus: "I will breathe in, conscious of the whole breath-body". He trains himself thus: "I will breathe out, conscious of the whole breath-body". He trains himself, thinking "I will breathe in, calming the whole bodily process". He trains himself, thinking "I will breathe out, calming the whole bodily process". Just as a skilled turner or his apprentice, in making a long turn, knows that he is making a long turn, or in making a short turn, knows that he is making a short turn, so too a bhikkhu understands that he breathes in a long breath. . . . So he trains himself, thinking "I will breathe out, calming the whole bodily process".'

5. 'So he abides contemplating the body as body internally, or contemplating the body as body externally, or contemplating the body as body both internally and externally.[5] He abides contemplating arising phenomena[6] in the body, he abides contemplating

vanishing phenomena in the body, he abides contemplating arising and vanishing phenomena in the body.[7] Or else, mindfulness that "there is a body" is present, to the extent necessary for knowledge and awareness. And he abides independent, not clinging to anything in the world. That, bhikkhus, is how a bhikkhu abides contemplating the body as body.'

II. *The Four Postures*

6. 'Again, when walking, a bhikkhu knows "I am walking"; when standing he knows "I am standing"; when sitting he knows "I am sitting"; when lying down he knows "I am lying down". In whatever way his body is disposed, he knows that that is how it is.

7. 'So he abides contemplating the body as body internally, externally, and both internally and externally. He abides contemplating arising phenomena in the body, he abides contemplating vanishing phenomena in the body, he abides contemplating both arising and vanishing phenomena in the body. Or else, mindfulness that "there is a body" is present, to the extent necessary for knowledge and awareness. And he abides independent, not clinging to anything in the world. That, bhikkhus, is how a bhikkhu abides contemplating the body as body.'

III. *Clear Awareness*

8. 'Again, a bhikkhu, when going forward or back, is clearly aware of what he is doing; in looking forward or back he is clearly aware of what he is doing; in bending and stretching he is clearly aware of what he is doing; in carrying his inner and outer robe and his bowl he is clearly aware of what he is doing; in eating,

drinking, chewing and savouring he is clearly aware of what he is doing; in passing excrement or urine he is clearly aware of what he is doing; in walking, standing, sitting, falling asleep and waking up, in speaking or in staying silent, he is clearly aware of what he is doing.

9. 'So he abides contemplating the body as body internally, externally, and both internally and externally. He abides contemplating arising phenomena in the body, he abides contemplating vanishing phenomena in the body, he abides contemplating both arising and vanishing phenomena in the body. Or else, mindfulness that "there is a body" is present, to the extent necessary for knowledge and awareness. And he abides independent, not clinging to anything in the world. That, bhikkhus, is how a bhikkhu abides contemplating the body as body.'

IV. *Reflection on the Repulsive: Parts of the Body*

10. 'Again, a bhikkhu reviews this very body from the soles of the feet upwards and from the scalp downwards, enclosed by skin and full of many kinds of impurities: "In this body there are head-hairs, body-hairs, nails, teeth, skin, flesh, sinews, bones, marrow, kidneys, heart, liver, diaphragm,[8] spleen, lungs, large intestine, small intestine, contents of the stomach, excrement, bile, phlegm, pus, blood, sweat, fat, tears, tallow, saliva, snot, fluid of the joints, and urine".[9] Just as if there were a bag, open at both ends, full of various kinds of grain such as hill-rice, red rice, beans, peas, millet, white rice, and a man with good eyesight were to open the bag and examine them, saying: "This is hill-rice, this is red rice, these are beans, these are peas, this is millet, this is white rice", so too a bhikkhu reviews this very body: "In this body there are head-hair . . . urine".

11. 'So he abides contemplating the body as body internally, externally, and both internally and externally. He abides contemplating arising phenomena in the body, he abides contemplating vanishing phenomena in the body, he abides contemplating both arising and vanishing phenomena in the body. Or else, mindfulness that "there is a body" is present, to the extent necessary for knowledge and awareness. And he abides independent, not clinging to anything in the world. That, bhikkhus, is how a bhikkhu abides contemplating the body as body.'

V. *The Four Elements*

12. 'Again, a bhikkhu reviews this body, however it may be placed or disposed, in terms of the elements: "There are in this body the earth element, the water element, the fire element, the air element". Just as if a skilled butcher or his apprentice, having slaughtered a cow, were to sit at a cross-roads with the carcass divided into portions, so a bhikkhu reviews this very body, however it may be placed or disposed, in terms of the elements: "There are in this body the earth element, the water element, the fire element, the air element".

13. 'So he abides contemplating the body as body internally, externally, and both internally and externally. He abides contemplating arising phenomena in the body, he abides contemplating vanishing phenomena in the body, he abides contemplating both arising and vanishing phenomena in the body. Or else, mindfulness that "there is a body" is present, to the extent necessary for knowledge and awareness. And he abides independent, not clinging to anything in the world. That, bhikkhus, is how a bhikkhu abides contemplating the body as body.'

VI. *The Nine Charnel Ground Contemplations*[10]

14. 'Again, a bhikkhu, as if he were to see a corpse thrown aside in a charnel ground, one, two or three days dead, bloated, discoloured, festering, compares this body with that, thinking "This body [of mine] is of the same nature, it will become like that, it is not exempt from that fate".

15. 'So he abides contemplating the body as body internally, externally, and both internally and externally. He abides contemplating arising phenomena in the body, contemplating vanishing phenomena in the body, he abides contemplating both arising and vanishing phenomena in the body. Or else, mindfulness that "there is a body" is present, to the extent necessary for knowledge and awareness. And he abides independent, not clinging to anything in the world. That, bhikkhus, is how a bhikkhu abides contemplating the body as body.

16. 'Again, a bhikkhu, as if he were to see a corpse in a charnel ground, thrown aside, eaten by crows, hawks or vultures, dogs or jackals, or various other creatures, compares this body with that, thinking "This body [of mine] is of the same nature, it will become like that, it is not exempt from that fate".

17. 'So he abides contemplating the body as body internally, externally, and both internally and externally. He abides contemplating arising phenomena in the body, contemplating vanishing phenomena in the body, he abides contemplating both arising and vanishing phenomena in the body. Or else, mindfulness that "there is a body" is present, to the extent necessary for knowledge and awareness. And he abides independent, not clinging to anything in the world. That, bhikkhus, is how a bhikkhu abides contemplating the body as body.

18–24. 'Again, a bhikkhu, as if he were to see a corpse in a charnel ground, thrown aside, a skeleton with flesh and blood,
connected by sinews . . . a fleshless skeleton smeared with blood,
connected by sinews . . . a skeleton without flesh and blood,
connected by sinews . . . disconnected bones, scattered in all di-
rections, a hand-bone here, a foot-bone there, a shin-bone here, a
thigh-bone there, a hip-bone here, a back-bone there, a rib-bone
here, a breast-bone there, an arm-bone here, a shoulder-bone
there, a neck-bone here, a jaw-bone there, here a tooth, there a
skull, compares this body with that, thinking "This body [of
mine] is of the same nature, it will become like that, it is not exempt from that fate".

25. 'So he abides contemplating the body as body internally,
externally, and both internally and externally. He abides contemplating arising phenomena in the body, contemplating vanishing
phenomena in the body, he abides contemplating both arising and
vanishing phenomena in the body. Or else, mindfulness that
"there is a body" is present, to the extent necessary for knowledge
and awareness. And he abides independent, not clinging to anything in the world. That is how a bhikkhu abides contemplating
the body as body.

26–30. 'Again, a bhikkhu, as if he were to see a corpse in a charnel ground, thrown aside, the bones whitened, looking like shells
. . . the bones piled up, a year old . . . the bones rotted away to a
powder, compares this body with that, thinking "This body [of
mine] is of the same nature, it will become like that, it is not exempt from that fate".'

31. 'So he abides contemplating the body as body internally,
externally, and both internally and externally. He abides contemplating arising phenomena in the body, contemplating vanishing
phenomena in the body, he abides contemplating both arising and

vanishing phenomena in the body. Or else, mindfulness that "there is a body" is present to him, to the extent necessary for knowledge and awareness. And he abides independent, not clinging to anything in the world. That, bhikkhus, is how a bhikkhu abides contemplating the body as body.'

MINDFULNESS OF FEELINGS
(*vedanānupassanā*)

32. 'And how bhikkhus, does a bhikkhu abide contemplating feelings as feelings? Here [in this teaching] when feeling a pleasant feeling, a bhikkhu knows "I feel a pleasant feeling"; when feeling a painful feeling, he knows "I feel a painful feeling"; when feeling a feeling that is neither painful nor pleasant, he knows "I feel a neither painful nor pleasant feeling". When feeling a pleasant sensual feeling, he knows "I feel a pleasant sensual feeling"; when feeling a pleasant non-sensual feeling[1], he knows "I am feeling a pleasant non-sensual feeling". When feeling a painful sensual feeling, he knows "I am feeling a painful sensual feeling"; when feeling a painful non-sensual feeling, he knows "I am feeling a painful non-sensual feeling". When feeling a sensual feeling that is neither painful nor pleasant, he knows "I am feeling a sensual feeling that is neither painful nor pleasant"; when feeling a non-sensual feeling that is neither painful nor pleasant, he knows "I am feeling a non-sensual feeling that is neither painful nor pleasant".'

33. 'So he abides contemplating feelings as feelings internally, he abides contemplating feelings as feelings externally, and he abides contemplating feelings as feelings both internally and externally. He abides contemplating arising phenomena in the feelings, vanishing phenomena in the feelings, and both arising and vanishing phenomena in the feelings. Or else, mindfulness that "there is feeling" is present, to the extent necessary for knowledge

and awareness. And he abides independent, not clinging to anything in the world. That, bhikkhus, is how a bhikkhu abides contemplating feelings as feelings.'

MINDFULNESS OF THINKING AND OF MIND
(*cittānupassanā*)

34. 'And how, bhikkhus, does a bhikkhu abide contemplating thinking as thinking? Here [in this teaching] a bhikkhu knows thinking affected by lust as thinking affected by lust, and thought free from lust as free from lust; thinking affected by hate as thinking affected by hate, and thought free from hate as free from hate; a deluded mind as deluded, an undeluded mind as undeluded; a contracted mind as contracted;[12] a distracted mind as distracted; a developed mind as developed, an undeveloped mind as undeveloped; a surpassed mind as surpassed, an unsurpassed mind as unsurpassed;[13] a concentrated mind as concentrated, an unconcentrated mind as unconcentrated; a liberated mind as liberated, an unliberated mind as unliberated.'

35. 'So he abides contemplating mind as mind internally, he abides contemplating mind as mind externally,[14] and he abides contemplating mind as mind both internally and externally. He abides contemplating arising phenomena in the mind, vanishing phenomena in the mind, and both arising and vanishing phenomena in the mind. Or else, mindfulness that "there is thinking" is present to the extent necessary for knowledge and awareness. And he abides independent, not clinging to anything in the world. That, bhikkhus, is how a bhikkhu abides contemplating mind as mind.'

MINDFULNESS OF DHAMMAS[15]
(*dhammānupassanā*)

36. 'And how, bhikkhus, does a bhikkhu abide contemplating dhammas as dhammas?'

I. *The Five Hindrances*

'Here [in this teaching] a bhikkhu abides contemplating dhammas as dhammas in terms of the five hindrances.[16] How does a bhikkhu contemplate dhammas as dhammas in terms of the five hindrances? Here bhikkhus, if worldly desire is present in him, a bhikkhu knows "There is worldly desire in me"; if worldly desire is absent in him, he knows "There is no worldly desire in me". And he knows how unarisen worldly desire comes to arise, and he knows how abandonment of arisen worldly desire comes about, and he knows how to prevent the arising of abandoned worldly desire in the future.

'If ill will[17] is present in him, a bhikkhu knows "There is ill will in me" . . . And he knows how to prevent the arising of abandoned ill will in the future.

'If laziness and dullness are present in him, a bhikkhu knows "There are laziness and dullness in me". . . And he knows how to prevent the arising of abandoned laziness and dullness in the future.

'If restlessness and worry are present in him, a bhikkhu knows "There are restlessness and worry in me". . . And he knows how to prevent the arising of abandoned restlessness and worry in the future.

'If doubt is present in him, a bhikkhu knows "There is doubt in me"; if doubt is absent, he knows: "There is no doubt in me". And he knows how arisen doubt comes to arise, and he knows how abandonment of arisen doubt comes about, and he knows how to prevent the arising of abandoned doubt in the future.'

37. 'So he abides contemplating dhammas as dhammas internally, externally, and both internally and externally. He abides contemplating arising phenomena in dhammas, contemplating vanishing phenomena in dhammas, and contemplating both arising and vanishing phenomena in dhammas. Or else mindfulness that "there are dhammas" is present, to the extent necessary for knowledge and awareness. And he abides independent, not clinging to anything in the world. That, bhikkhus, is how a bhikkhu abides contemplating dhammas as dhammas in terms of the five hindrances.'

II. *The Five Aggregates*

38. 'Again, bhikkhus, a bhikkhu abides contemplating dhammas as dhammas in terms of the five aggregates of clinging. How does a bhikkhu contemplate dhammas as dhammas in terms of the five aggregates of clinging ? Here [in this teaching] a bhikkhu knows "Such is form, such the arising of form, such the disappearance of form; such is feeling, such the arising of feeling, such the disappearance of feeling; such is perception, such the arising of perception, such the disappearance of perception; such are the mental formations, such the arising of mental formations, such the disappearance of mental formations; such is consciousness, such the arising of consciousness, such the disappearance of consciousness".'

39. 'So he abides contemplating dhammas as dhammas internally, externally, and both internally and externally. He abides contemplating arising phenomena in dhammas, contemplating vanishing phenomena in dhammas, and contemplating arising and vanishing phenomena in dhammas. Or else mindfulness that "there are dhammas" is present, to the extent necessary for knowledge and awareness. And he abides independent, not grasping at

anything in the world. That, bhikkhus, is how a bhikkhu abides contemplating dhammas as dhammas in terms of the five aggregates of clinging.'

III. *The Six Internal and External Sense-Bases*

40. 'Again, bhikkhus, a bhikkhu abides contemplating dhammas as dhammas in terms of the six internal and external sense-bases. How does a bhikkhu contemplate dhammas as dhammas in terms of the six internal and external sense-bases? Here [in this teaching] a bhikkhu knows the eye, he knows visible forms, and he knows whatever fetter arises dependent on both. And he knows how an unarisen fetter comes to arise, and he knows how abandonment of an arisen fetter comes about, and he knows how to prevent the arising of an abandoned fetter in the future.

'He knows the ear, and knows sounds . . .

'He knows the nose, and knows smells . . .

'He knows the tongue, and knows tastes . . .

'He knows the body, and knows physical contacts . . .

'He knows the mind, and knows dhammas, and he knows whatever fetter arises dependent on both. And he knows how an unarisen fetter comes to arise, and he knows how abandonment of an arisen fetter comes about, and he knows how to prevent the arising of an abandoned fetter in the future.'

41. 'So he abides contemplating dhammas as dhammas internally, externally, and both internally and externally. He abides contemplating arising phenomena in dhammas, contemplating vanishing phenomena in dhammas, and contemplating arising and vanishing phenomena in dhammas. Or else mindfulness that "there are dhammas" is present, to the extent necessary for knowledge and awareness. And he abides independent, not grasping at anything in the world. That, bhikkhus, is how a bhikkhu abides

contemplating dhammas as dhammas in terms of the six internal and external sense-bases.'

IV. *The Seven Factors of Enlightenment*

42. 'Again, bhikkhus, a bhikkhu abides contemplating dhammas as dhammas in terms of the seven factors of enlightenment. How does a bhikkhu contemplate dhammas as dhammas in terms of the seven factors of enlightenment? Here [in this teaching], if the factor of mindfulness is present in him, a bhikkhu knows "There is the enlightenment factor of mindfulness in me"; if the factor of mindfulness is not present in him, he knows "The enlightenment factor of mindfulness is absent in me". And he knows how the unarisen factor of mindfulness comes to arise, and he knows how the complete development of the factor of mindfulness comes about.

'If the enlightenment factor of investigation of dhammas is present in him . . .

'If the enlightenment factor of energy is present in him . . .

'If the enlightenment factor of delight is present in him . . .

'If the enlightenment factor of tranquillity is present in him . . .

'If the enlightenment factor of concentration is present in him . . .

'If the enlightenment factor of equanimity is present in him, a bhikkhu knows "There is the enlightenment factor of equanimity in me"; if the factor of equanimity is not present in him, he knows "The enlightenment factor of equanimity is absent in me". And he knows how the unarisen factor of equanimity comes to arise, and he knows how the complete development of the factor of equanimity comes about.'

43. 'So he abides contemplating dhammas as dhammas internally, externally, and both internally and externally. He abides

contemplating arising phenomena in dhammas, contemplating vanishing phenomena in dhammas, and contemplating arising and vanishing phenomena in dhammas. Or else mindfulness that "there are dhammas" is present, to the extent necessary for knowledge and awareness. And he abides independent, not grasping at anything in the world. That, bhikkhus, is how a bhikkhu abides contemplating dhammas as dhammas in terms of the seven factors of enlightenment.'

V. *The Four Noble Truths*

44. 'Again, bhikkhus, a bhikkhu abides contemplating dhammas as dhammas in terms of the Four Noble Truths. How does a bhikkhu contemplate dhammas as dhammas in terms of the Four Noble Truths? Here [in this teaching] a bhikkhu knows as it really is: "This is suffering"; he knows as it really is: "This is the origin of suffering"; he knows as it really is: "This is the cessation of suffering"; he knows as it really is: "This is the way of practice[18] leading to the cessation of suffering".'

45. 'So he abides contemplating dhammas as dhammas internally, externally, and both internally and externally. He abides contemplating arising phenomena in dhammas, contemplating vanishing phenomena in dhammas, and contemplating arising and vanishing phenomena in dhammas. Or else mindfulness that "there are dhammas" is present, to the extent necessary for knowledge and awareness. And he abides independent, not grasping at anything in the world. That, bhikkhus, is how a bhikkhu abides contemplating dhammas as dhammas in terms of the Four Noble Truths.'

CONCLUSION

46. 'Bhikkhus, if anyone should practise these four foundations of mindfulness in such a way for seven years, he may expect one of two fruits: either arahatship in this life or, if there is a trace of clinging left, the state of non-returner.[19]

'Let alone seven years. If anyone should practise them for six years . . . , for five years . . . , for four years . . . , for three years . . . , for two years . . . , for one year, he may expect one of two fruits . . .

'Let alone one year. If anyone should practise them for seven months . . . , for six months . . . , for five months . . . , for four months . . . , for three months . . . , for two months . . . , for one month . . . , for half a month, he may expect one of two fruits . . .

'Let alone half a month. If anyone should develop these four foundations of mindfulness for seven days, he may expect one of two fruits: either arahatship in this life or, if there is a trace of clinging left, the state of non-returner.

47. 'So it was with reference to this that it was said: "This is, bhikkhus, the direct path for the purification of beings, for the overcoming of sorrow and distress, for the disappearance of pain and sadness, for reaching the right path, for the realisation of *nibbāna* – namely the four foundations of mindfulness".'

This is what the Blessed One said. The bhikkhus rejoiced and were delighted at his words.

NOTES

1. Although this discourse is directed to monks or *bhikkhus*, it does not mean that these foundations are only meant for them. This paragraph indicates that this is indeed not the intention of the Buddha, because these foundations lead to the purification of all beings. The Commentary says that the term is used to include anyone who undertakes this practice.

2. 'Body as body' means that during the meditation practice, the body is not confused with feelings, thoughts and the like. The body is also not seen as 'my body', as 'mine', or as 'me'. It is merely seen as a phenomenon.
'Hankering and fretting' in the next line refer to the hindrances of desire and ill will, which have to be overcome for the practice to succeed. See also verse 36.

3. The word *dhamma* has several meanings, depending on the context in which it is used. It can mean: natural phenomenon, mental object, truth, reality, wisdom or (skilful) action. Sometimes the term '*dhammas*' is used in the context of the four foundations of mindfulness. *Dhamma* with a capital D can refer to the teachings of the Buddha or to the scriptures that contain these teachings. In the context of this *sutta*, *dhamma* means any natural phenomenon, in particular the five hindrances, the five aggregates of clinging, the six inner and outer sense-bases, the seven factors of enlightenment, and the Four Noble Truths.

4. What is described here is a mental exercise in mindfulness, and not an exercise in controlling the breath as in certain yoga practices.

5. Internally means 'one's own body', externally means 'someone else's body'. The insight that is developed through the observation of someone else's body is more reflective in nature.

6. In the Pali text *samudaya* is used for 'arising', a word that can also be used in the sense of 'cause' or 'origin'. *Samudaya-sacca* is the second noble truth, namely 'the truth that there is a cause of suffering'. In this *sutta*, *samudaya dhamma* is used to mean awareness of how phenomena (body, etc.) come to be.

7. By being mindful of the arising and passing away of phenomena, the three universal characteristics of all living beings become clearly recognisable: impermanence, unsatisfactoriness and uncontrollability.

8. This term includes other pleura that keep all the different parts of the body in place.

9. In later texts the brain is added to the above list to form thirty-two parts. The details of the meditation on the thirty-two parts of the body are explained in the *Visuddhimagga*.

10. These are places where rotting corpses were taken to decompose. In India such places were also used as *samvega-vatthu*, an encouragement to come to non-attachment as regards life and death.

11. For example the beneficial results of practising meditation.

12. 'Contracted' or 'shrunken' by laziness and dullness. 'Distracted' in the next pair is caused by restlessness and worry.

13. Developed and undeveloped mind are terms used to indicate a mind that has developed deep concentration (*jhāna* in various stages), and mind that has not developed concentration. Surpassed mind means 'having (other mental states) surpassing it', synonymous with the 'undeveloped mind'. Unsurpassed mind means 'having no other states surpassing it', synonymous with 'developed mind'.

14. Through inference and reflection, as well as through using knowledge of others.

15. See note 3 for the meanings of the word *dhamma*.

16. 'Hindrance' is to be understood primarily as an obstacle that pulls someone into the stream of desire, hatred and delusion, and keeps them there. From the moment there is mindfulness of these hindrances they are no longer a hindrance, but they are transformed into valuable meditation objects.

17. Ill will also means hatred, aversion, resentment, anger, resistance and the like.

18. This is the Eightfold Path.

19. This means that a patient practitioner can become an *arahat*, someone who has realised the highest stage of enlightenment. If there are still traces of attachment present, that person is called an *anāgāmi*, a once-returner. According to the scriptures, *anāgāmis* are completely free from hatred and sense desire. But because there are still some slight attachments, they will be reborn in a realm of existence that is invisible and conditioned in a subtler way, and realise the highest phase of enlightenment in that realm.

APPENDIX II

ENGAGED BUDDHISM

'Engaged Buddhism' is a recent development – on a global scale – in Buddhism, that arose from a sense of compassion and justice. This movement was formalised in 1989 during a conference in Thailand, when thirty-six lay people and monastics (from eleven countries) founded INEB, the International Network of Engaged Buddhists. The aims of INEB are:

- Being a concrete manifestation of engaged Buddhism
- Promoting inter-Buddhist and inter-religious collaboration and understanding
- Providing information on Buddhism and other socially active groups
- Organising meetings on INEB's areas of interest

At present INEB has more than 350 active members and active working groups in thirty-three countries. From this diversity it is working towards a growing understanding of commitment, where the spiritual practice of meditation and study is integrated with social action, and of service to a healthy, just and peaceful world. This social engagement is based on universal wisdom and compassion. INEB is involved in education, human rights, environmental issues, women's rights, collaboration between developing and developed countries, and relating spirituality to social action. Over time the network has organised various workshops. Central to these workshops are social awareness, non-violent conflict resolution, promoting peace in general, and advocating the rights of the oppressed. INEB has established and supported many projects, and publishes a magazine called *Seeds of Peace* three times a year.

His Holiness the Dalai Lama (who was awarded the Nobel Peace Prize) is one of the patrons of INEB. Other prominent Buddhists who are involved are the Vietnamese Buddhist monk Thich Nhat Hanh, Venerable Mahāghosananda from Cambodia, and the Thai social and peace activist Sulak Sivaraksa (these three have been nominated for the Nobel Peace Prize). The American monk Phra Santikaro and the English meditation teacher Christopher Titmuss are also connected with INEB, amongst many others.

Besides INEB there are many other Buddhist groups which support or initiate projects dealing with human pain and suffering. Wat Tham Krabok is a good example: the previous abbot of this Thai monastery has developed a very successful detoxification programme for drug addicts. Another example is Wat Phra Bat Nam Phu in Lopburi (Thailand), where people suffering from AIDS are cared for.

For more information about INEB and other socially engaged groups or projects, see the addresses in appendix 4 under 'Thailand'.

APPENDIX III

GLOSSARY

Abhidhamma: literally 'higher doctrine', one of the three parts of the *Tipitaka* (the *Abhidhamma* texts are specifically concerned with Buddhist psychology).

Ahāra: source of life. There are four *āhāras*:
1. the law of cause and effect (*kamma*),
2. consciousness (*citta*),
3. climate, temperature (*utu*),
4. physical nourishment (*āhāra*).

Akusala: unwholesome

Anāgāmi: literally 'non-returner', indicating someone who has realised the third stage of enlightenment.

Anattā: egolessness, no self, uncontrollability, ungovernability or unpredictability. One of the three universal characteristics of existence.

Anicca: impermanence, changeability. One of the three characteristics of existence.

Anusaya: latent impurity of mind, inherent in human existence. There are seven *anusayas*:
1. sensual desire (*kāmarāga*),
2. the urge to be or become something or someone (*bhavarāga*),
3. aggression, anger, hatred (*patigha*),
4. pride, arrogance (*māna*),
5. mistaken view, misunderstanding (*ditthi*),
6. doubt, uncertainty (*vicikicchā*),
7. ignorance (*avijjā*).

Arahat: literally 'purified one', indicating someone who has realised the fourth and final stage of enlightenment. The impurities of mind have been completely eradicated.

Asura: jealous demigod, symbol of the realm of jealousy.

Attā (or *atman*): 'self', soul or ego.

Avijjā: ignorance, misunderstanding, delusion, unconsciousness as regards what is happening in or to us here and now.

Ayoniso manasikāra: unwise interpretation or one that is not based on wisdom, in dealing with what is happening in the present moment, caused by not being aware and by carelessness.

Bala: (potential) power, meaning the five *indriyas* at a deeper level.

Bhavatanhā: urge to be or become somebody or something (literally: craving for existence).

Bhikkhu: Buddhist monk.

Bhikkhuni: Buddhist nun.

Bodhisattva: someone striving for enlightenment, developing certain perfections of mind, such as generosity, patience and wisdom (Pali: *bodhisatta*).

Brahmavihāra: sublime states of mind (literally: divine abodes). There are four *brahmavihāras*:

1. lovingkindness (*mettā*),
2. compassion (*karunā*),
3. sympathetic joy (*muditā*),
4. equanimity (*upekkhā*).

Buddha: title for someone who has awakened from the ignorance or delusion caused by not seeing reality clearly.

Cittānupassanā: the third of the four foundations of mindfulness, namely mindfulness of thinking, and of the mind.

Deva: divine being, living in the realm of sensual bliss.

Dhamma: the teachings of the Buddha.

Dhamma(s): natural phenomena, mental object, a state, truth, reality, wisdom, action, skilful action or practice.

Dhammānupassanā: the last of the four foundations for the cultivation of mindfulness, namely mindfulness of mental and physical phenomena in general. Those specifically mentioned in this context are: the five hindrances, the five aggregates of clinging, the six inner and outer sense bases, the seven factors of enlightenment, and the four Noble Truths.

Dhamma vicaya: intuitive investigation of phenomena, penetrating insight.

Dhutanga: ascetic practice.

Dukkha: the most conventional translation is 'suffering', the most accurate translation for me is 'unsatisfactoriness'. Other renderings are: pain, conflict, frustration, instability, insecurity or burden. The first Noble Truth and one of the three universal characteristics of existence.

Dukkha sacca: the first Noble Truth, the 'truth that there is suffering'.

Hetu: driving force for wholesome or unwholesome karma.

Indriya: wholesome power or factor that is developed by means of *vipassanā* meditation (literally: controlling faculty). There are five *indriyas*:

1. confidence (*saddhā*),
2. effort (*viriya*),
3. mindfulness (*sati*),
4. concentration (*samādhi*),
5. wisdom (*paññā*).

Jhāna: deep level of absorption or concentration.

Kāmacchanda: sensual pleasure and desire. One of the five *nivaraṇa*.

Kāmatanhā: sensual desire.

Karma: the law of cause and effect (Pali: *kamma*).

Karunā: compassion. One of the four *brahmavihāras*.

Kāyānupassanā: the first of the four foundations of mindfulness, namely mindfulness of the body.

Khema: state of security, safety and stability (this term is used to describe enlightenment).

Kilesa: impurity, taint or defilement of the mind. There are ten *kilesa*:

1. desire and attachment (*lobha*),
2. hatred (*dosa*),
3. ignorance or lack of understanding of reality (*moha*),
4. pride and self-righteousness (*māna*),
5. wrong view of reality (*ditthi*),
6. sceptical doubt, uncertainty (*vicikicch*),

7. laziness and dullness (*thina*),
8. restlessness (*uddhacca*),
9. absence of moral shame (*ahirika*),
10. absence of moral fear (of criticism) (*anottappa*).

Kusala: wholesome.

Loka: realm or sphere of consciousness.

Magga-citta: path-consciousness. A form of supramundane consciousness.

Magga-sacca: the fourth Noble Truth, the 'truth of the way leading to the cessation of suffering, namely the Eightfold Path', consisting of:

1. right understanding (*sammā ditthi*),
2. right thought (*sammā sankappa*),
3. right speech (*sammā vāccā*),
4. right action (*sammā kammanta*),
5. right livelihood (*sammā ājiva*),
6. right effort (*sammā vāyāma*),
7. right mindfulness (*sammā sati*),
8. right concentration (*sammā samādhi*).

Mahāyāna: literally 'great vehicle'. A school in Buddhism that developed later.

Mantra: sound, word or phrase as object of meditation.

Māra: literally 'the killer of virtue, destroyer of that which is wholesome'. Māra is the Buddhist equivalent of Satan, and is symbolic of all the temptations we can encounter on the path of meditation. The ten armies of Māra are:

1. sensual pleasure and attachment (*kāma*),
2. dissatisfaction (*arati*),
3. hunger and thirst (*khuppipāsā*),
4. desire (*tanhā*),
5. laziness and sleepiness (*thina-middha*),
6. fear (*bhiru*),
7. doubt (*vicikicchā*),
8. hypocrisy and conceitedness (*makkha* and *thambha*),
9. gain, fame and honour (*lābha*, *siloka* and *sakkāra*),

10. self-glorification and demeaning of others (*attukkamsana* and *paravambhana*).

Mettā: lovingkindness. One of the four *brahmavihāras*.

Mettā-bhāvanā: the cultivation or practice of lovingkindness.

Muditā: sympathetic joy. One of the four *brahmavihāras*.

Nibbāna: literally 'not or no longer blowing or burning'. This term is used to indicate the state of enlightenment.

Nirodha sacca: the third Noble Truth, the 'truth of the cessation of suffering'. This is realised through the experience of *nibbāna*.

Nivarana: hindrance. There are five *nivaranas*:

1. sensual pleasure and desire (*kāmacchanda*),
2. hatred, anger or aversion (*byāpāda*),
3. laziness, dullness, sleepiness (*thina-middha*),
4. restlessness and worry (*uddhacca-kukkucca*),
5. doubt or uncertainty (*vicikicchā*).

Pali: the language used in the oldest Buddhist scriptures.

Paññā: wisdom, liberating insight.

Pārami: perfection of mind (Sanskrit: *pāramitā*). In the *Theravāda* texts ten *pārami* are mentioned:

1. generosity (*dāna*),
2. virtue (*sila*),
3. renunciation or restraint (*nekkhamma*),
4. wisdom (*paññā*),
5. diligence, determination, effort (*viriya*),
6. patience (*khanti*),
7. truthfulness (*sacca*),
8. perseverance (*adhitthāna*),
9. lovingkindness (*mettā*),
10. equanimity (*upekkhā*).

Phala-citta: fruition-consciousness. A type of supramundane consciousness.

Peta: hungry ghost, symbolic for the world of unfulfilled desire (Sanskrit: *preta*).

Sakadāgāmi: literally 'once-returner', indicating someone who has realised the second stage of enlightenment.

Samādhi: meditation; concentration or one-pointedness of mind. There are three kinds of *samādhi*:

1. 'approaching' concentration or access concentration (*upacāra-samādhi*),
2. deep, complete concentration (*appanā-samādhi*),
3. momentary concentration (*khanika-samādhi*).

Sāmanera: Buddhist novice or student-monk.

Samatha: tranquillity, calm, relaxation.

Sammohavinodani: title of an important commentary in *Theravāda* Buddhism.

Samsāra: cycle of birth and rebirth, also called the wheel of life or 'the merry-go-round'.

Samudaya sacca: the second Noble Truth, the 'truth that there is a cause of suffering, namely desire'.

Samvega-vatthu: object or sign that evokes a sense of spiritual urgency.

Samyojana: constricting driving force, 'fetter'. There are ten *samyojanas*:

1. sensual desire (*kāmarāga*),
2. hatred (*pathiga*),
3. pride, conceit (*māna*),
4. mistaken view (*ditthi*),
5. unrealistic belief in rites and rituals (*silabbātaparamāsa*),
6. doubt, scepticism (*vicikicchā*),
7. clinging to *jhāna* and its fruits (*bhavarāga*),
8. jealousy (*issā*),
9. miserliness (*macchariya*),
10. misunderstanding, delusion, ignorance (*avijjā*).

Sangha: community of monks, nuns and lay followers of the Buddha and the Dhamma.

Santi: peace (a description of enlightenment).

Satipatthāna: foundation of mindfulness.

Sila: morality, virtue, ethics, discipline. There are three kinds of *sila*:

1. elementary ethics (*varitta sila*),
2. refined or elaborated ethics (*caritta sila*),
3. the discipline that protects the senses (*indriya samvara sila*).

Sotāpanna: literally 'streamwinner', a description of someone who has realised the first stage of enlightenment.

Sutta: teaching or discourse of the Buddha. The whole body of Suttas form the first part of the *Tipitaka.*

Theravāda: literally 'advice of the elders', indicating the original form of Buddhism. Later on *Mahāyāna* and Tibetan Buddhism emerged from *Theravāda.*

Tilakkhana: the three universal characteristics of existence, namely impermanence, unsatisfactoriness and uncontrollability.

Tipiṭaka: literally 'the three baskets'. It indicates the Buddhist scriptures, comprising of three divisions, namely the Vinaya, the Suttas and the Abhidhamma.

Ummattaka: the state of madness, having lost one's senses or being very disturbed. There are eight causes of *ummattaka:*

1. desire *(kāmummattaka),*
2. hatred, anger *(kodhummattaka),*
3. mistaken view *(ditthummattaka),*
4. ignorance *(mohummattaka).*
5. negative external influences[1] *(yakkhummattaka),*
6. organic and hormonal irregularities *(pittummattaka),*
7. intoxicating, addictive substances *(surummattaka),*
8. devastating loss or mishap *(vyāsanummattaka).*

Upakilesa: taint, defilement or pitfall in the development of insight. Because of the last *upakilesa* they turn into pitfalls. There are ten *upakilesas* that can arise during the practice of insight meditation:

1. seeing light or colours *(obhāsa),*
2. insight *(ñāna),*
3. rapture *(pīti),*
4. serenity *(passaddhi),*
5. happiness, contentment *(sukha),*
6. confidence, determination *(adhimokkha),*
7. energy *(paggāha),*
8. strong mindfulness, clarity *(upatthāna),*
9. equanimity *(upekkhā),*

10. clinging, attachment (*nikanti*).

Upekkhā: equanimity. One of the four *brahmavihāras*.

Vajrayāna: literally 'the diamond vehicle', indicating a later form of Buddhism, popularly known as Tibetan Buddhism.

Vedanānupassanā: the second of the four foundations or bases for the cultivation of mindfulness, namely mindfulness of feelings.

Vibhavatanhā: urge to destroy.

Vimamsā: wisdom.

Vimutti: liberation (a description of enlightenment).

Vinaya: morality, ethics. One of the three parts of the *Tipitaka*.

Vipāka: result, effect, the fruit of karma.

Vipallāsa: illusion, 'mirage'.

Vipassanā: insight, liberating insight, wisdom, intuitive understanding of reality as it is.

Visuddhi: (process of) purification. There are seven *visuddhis*:

1. purification of and through virtue (*sila-visuddhi*),
2. purification of consciousness (*citta-visuddhi*),
3. purification of the idea of 'self' (*ditthi-visuddhi*),
4. purification by transcending or overcoming doubt (*kankhā-vitarana-visuddhi*),
5. purification by knowledge and vision of what is the path and what not (*maggāmagga-ñānadassana-visuddhi*),
6. purification by knowledge and vision of the way (*patipadā-ñānadassana-visuddhi*),
7. purification by knowledge and insight (*ñānadassana-visuddhi*).

Visuddhimagga: the path of purification. A Sinhalese monk, Venerable Bhadantācariya Buddhaghosa wrote this book in about 400 A.D. by. It was translated into English by Bhikkhu Ñānamoli under the title *The Path of Purification*. The book is one of the most detailed handbooks of Buddhist meditation.

NOTES

1. Literally: demonic forces.

APPENDIX IV

USEFUL ADDRESSES

Addresses of *Vipassana* Meditation Centres and Contacts

AUSTRIA

- Buddhistische Kultusgemeinde, Fleischmarkt 16, A-1010 Vienna. Tel. 00-43-1-5123719.
- Buddhistischer Zentrum Scheibbs, Ginselberg 12, A-3270 Scheibbs-Neus. Tel. 00-43-7482-42412.

AUSTRALIA

- Blue Mountains Insight Meditation Centre, 25 Rutland Rd., Medlow Bath, NSW 2780.
  Tel. 00-61-2-4788-1024/4759-1443.
  Website: www.meditation.asn.au
  Email: bmimc@pmc.com.au or bmimc@mountains.net.au

BELGIUM

- Marie-Cécile Vandergucht, 2 Rue de la Duchesse, 1040 Brussels. Tel. 00-32-2-7341128.

BURMA (MYANMAR)

- Chanmyay Yeiktha Meditation Centre, 55a Kaba Aye Pagoda Road, Rangoon (Yangon) 11061.
  Tel. 00-95-1-661479. Fax 00-95-1-667050.
  Email: chanmyay@mptmail.net.mm
  Website: http://chanmyay.net
- Saddhammaransi Yeiktha, 7 Zeyar Khaymar Street, 8th mile, Mahayangon P.O., Rangoon (Yangon).
  Tel. 00-95-1-661597.

- Mahasi Tathana Yeiktha, 16 Tathana Yeiktha Road, Rangoon (Yangon) 11201. Tel. 00-95-1-541971, 552501. Fax 00-95-1-289960, 289961.
- Panditarama, 80a Thanlwin Road, Golden Hill Avenue, Bahan, Rangoon (Yangon). Tel. 00-95-1-531448. Fax 00-95-1-527171.

CANADA
- West Coast Dhamma Society, 2224 Larch St., Vancouver B.C., V6K 3P7. Tel. 00-1-604-731-5469.
- Manawmaya Theravada, 252 East 65th Ave., Vancouver B.C., V5X 2P4. Tel. 00-1-604-321-7634.
- Chanmyay Yeiktha Calgary, U Kitti, 69 Martin Valley Rd., Calgary. Tel. 00-1-403-568-7205.

CZECH REPUBLIC
- Dhamma Centrum Bodhipala, Vratislavska 386, schranka 6, 181 00 Praha 8. Tel. 00- 420-2-855-2203. Email: bodhipala@volny.cz Website: www.volny.cz/bodhipala

FRANCE
- Tapovan Forest Retreat, Marses, F-11300 Festes Tel. 00-33-468-318773. Email: tapovan@mac.com Website: www.dharmanetwork.org
- Sakyamuni Meditation Centre, Lieudit, Montbéon, St. Agnan, F- 89340 Villeneuve La Guyard. Tel. 00-33-8696-6332.
- Buddhist centre/temple: 6, Chemin de Boucharin, Tournon 7300 (near Lyon). Tel. 00-33-75-08-8669.

GERMANY
- Haus der Stille, Mühlenweg 20, D-21514 Roseburg (near Hamburg). Tel. 00-49-4158-214.
- Waldhaus am Laacher See, Heimschule 1, D-56645 Nickenich. Tel. 00-49-2636-3344. Fax 00-49-2636-2259. Email: budwest@t-online.de

USEFUL ADDRESSES

- Buddha-Haus, Uttenbühl 5, D-87466 Oy-Mittelberg.
  Tel. 00-49-8376-502. Fax 00-49-8376-592.
  Email: buddha-haus@t-online.de
  Website: www.buddha-haus.de

GREAT BRITAIN

- Gaia House, West Ogwell, Newton Abbot, Devon TQ12 6EN.
  Tel. 00-44-1626-333613. Website: www.gaiahouse.co.uk
- The Barn, Lower Sharpham Barton, Ashprington, Totness,
  Devon TQ9 7DX. Tel. 00-44-1803-732661.
  Email: college@sharpham-trust.org
  Website: www.sharpham-trust.org
- Bhikkhu Bodhidhamma. Email: info@satipanya.org.uk
  Website: www.satipanya.org.uk
- Burmese Vihara, 1, Old Church Lane, Wembley NW9 8TG.
  Tel. 00-44-181-200-6898.

INDIA

- Caroline Miller (after October 31, to register for January
  retreats), Poste Restante, Bodh Gaya, Gaya District, Bihar
  824231.
- Sarnath gatherings in February. For info see website
  www.insightmeditation.org

IRELAND

- Marjó Oosterhoff, 'Passaddhi', Leitrim Beg, Adrigole, Beara,
  Co. Cork. Tel. 00-353-27-60223.
  Email: moosterhoff@eircom.net
  Website: www.passaddhi.com
- Sunyata Retreat Centre, Belvoir Cross, Sixmilebridge, Co. Clare.
  Tel. 00-353-61-367073.
  Email: info@sunyatacentre.com
  Website: www.sunyatacentre.com

ISRAEL

- Dharma Gathering, Insight Society, P.O. Box 1479, 45114 Hod
  Hasharon. Tel. 00-972-53-432-217.

ITALY
- Ameco, Via Valle di Riva 1, 00141 Roma.
  Tel. 00-39-6-812-0138.
- Beatrice Taboga, Venice.
  Email: circolo.shanti@tiscalinet.it

JAPAN
- Theravada Buddhist Centre, Rose Haim 203 3-17-2 Mejiro,
  Tokyo 171. Tel. 00-81-3-3951-0390.

MALAYSIA
- Malaysian Buddhist Meditation Centre, 355 Jalan Masjid
  Negeri, 11600 Penang.

NEPAL
- Daw Dhammawati, Dhammakirti Vihar, Shreeyha, Naghal Tole,
  P.O. Box 4992, Kathmandu.

THE NETHERLANDS
- Vipassana Meditatie Centrum, Kamerlingh Onnessstraat 71,
  9727 HG Groningen. Tel. 00-31-50-5276051.
  Email: vipassana@castel.nl
  Website: www.stichtingen.castel.nl/vipassana
- Vipassana Meditatie Centrum Buddhavihara,
  St. Pieterspoortsteeg 29-I, 1012 HM Amsterdam.
  Tel. 020-6264984. Email: gotama@xs4all.nl
  Website: www.xs4all.nl/~gotama
- For events facilitated by Frits Koster, see www.fritskoster.nl

NEW ZEALAND
- Tauhara Insight Meditation, P.O. Box 125, Taupo.
  Tel. 00-64-7-378-750.
- Te Moata, P.O. Box 100, Tairua. Tel. 00-64-7-868-8798.
- Southern Insight Meditation, c/o Di Robertson, 16 Ward St.,
  Addington, Christchurch.

USEFUL ADDRESSES

PALESTINE
- Insight Society, P.O. Box 8747, 91086 Jerusalem.

POLAND
- Vipassana Alma Yoray, 58-563 Przesieka, UL Bukowy, GAJ4. Tel. 00-48-7-553-785.

RUSSIA
- St. Petersburg Theravada Association, Ul Gavanskaya 6-47, 199106 St. Petersburg.

SINGAPORE
- Vipassana Meditation, 5C-5D Jalan Haji Salam, 468748 Singapore. Tel. 00-65-2-4453-3984.

SOUTH AFRICA
- Buddhist Retreat Centre, P.O. Box 131, Ixopo3276, KwaZulu Natal. Tel. 00-27-39-8341-863.
  Email: brcixopo@futurenet.co.za
  Website: www.vanloon.co.za/brc
- DharmaGiri Retreat Centre (Thanissara & Kittisaro), P.O. Box 270, Underberg 3257, KwaZulu Natal. Tel. 00-27-33-7011-138. Email: dragonmtn@xsinet.co.za
- Myanmar Buddhist Association of South Africa, P.O. Box 22606, South Gate, Pietermaritzburg 3200.

SOUTH KOREA
- Bhante cho Amaranyano, 894-15 Chong Nung No. 4, Sam Jeong Sa.

SRI LANKA
- Vipassana Bhavana Centre, Kandubode, Delgoda. Tel. 00-94-445518.

SWEDEN
- Vipassana Group, Bjurhollmsplan, S-11663 Stockholm.

SWITZERLAND

- Meditation Center Beatenberg, CH-3802 Waldegg-Beatenberg
  Tel. 00-41-33-841-2131. Fax 00-41-33-841-2132.
  Website: www.karuna.ch

THAILAND

- Wat Mahadhatu (section 5), 3 Maharaj Road, Bangkok 10200.
  Tel. 00-66-2-222-6011.
- Wat Vivekasom, Soi Prachanakul 7, Thanon Banbung, Amphoe
  Mueang, Chonburi 20000. Tel. 00-66-38-283766.
- Wat Sorn Thawee, Sametnua, Bangkla, Chachoengsao 24110.
  Tel. 00-66-38-541405.
- Wat Kow Tahm, P.O. Box 18, Koh Phangan, Suratthani 84280.
  Website: www.watkowtham.org
- Dhammodaya Meditation Centre, 45/1 Mu 4, Tambon Thanon
  Khat, Amphoe Mueang, Nakhon Pathom 73000.
  Tel. 00-66-1-810-3692. Email: dhammodaya@hotmail.com
- Jeffrey Oliver (U Dhammarakhita), Wat Pichaiyat, Somdet
  Chaophraya Road, Klong San, Thonburi, Bangkok 10600.
  Tel. 00-66-1-777-9346. Email: udhamma@yahoo.com
- Sommitre Pranee Vipassana Centre, 118/1 Mu 1, Ban Nong
  Pru, Tambon Nong Pai Kaew, Amphoe Ban Beung, Chonburi
  Province 20220. Tel. 00-66-38-292-361, 00-66-1-343-7295.
  Email: wat_asabha@yahoo.com

ENGAGED BUDDHISM

- INEB (Internation Network of Engaged Buddhists, see appendix
  II), 124 Soi Wat Thongnopakhun, Somdej Chaopraya Rd.,
  Klong San, Thonburi, Bangkok 10600. Website: www.bpf.org/
  ineb.html, and www.sulak-sivaraksa.org/network22php
  Email: ineboffice@yahoo.com
- Wat Thamkrabok, Amphoe Koonklone, Phra Putthabat,
  Saraburi 18120. Website: www.thamkrabok.org
- Wat Phra Bat Nam Phu, Amphoe Mueang, Lopburi 15000.
  Website: www.aidstemple.th.org

USEFUL ADDRESSES

U.S.A.

- Insight Meditation Society, 1230 Pleasant Street, Barre,
  MA 01005. Tel. 00-1-978-355-4378.
  Website: www.dharma.org/ims.htm
- Spirit Rock Meditation Center, P.O. Box 169, Woodacre,
  CA 94973. Tel. 00-1-415-488-0164.
  Website: www.spiritrock.org
- Vipassana Hawai'i. Tel. 00-1-808-396-5888.
  Website: www.vipassanahawaii.org
- Vipassana Metta Foundation, P.O. Box 1188, Kula,
  HI 96790-1188. Tel. 00-1-808-573-3450.
  Email: metta@maui.net
  Website: www.vipassanametta.org

Tricycle magazine (www.tricycle.com) and *Inquiring Mind* (P.O. Box
9999, Berkeley CA 94709, www.inquiringmind.com) are good resources
for other addresses in the U.S. and Canada.

Please contact the author with changes or additional addresses:
info@fritskoster.nl.

APPENDIX V

RECOMMENDED READING

Bodhi, Bhikkhu, ed., *A Comprehensive Manual of Abhidhamma*, Buddhist Publication Society 1993.

———, *The Noble Eightfold Path*, Buddhist Publication Society 1994.

——— & Ñnamoli, Venerable, *The Middle Length Discourses of the Buddha (Majjhima Nikya)*, Wisdom 1995.

———, *The Connected Discourses of the Buddha (Samyutta Nikya)*, Wisdom 2000.

Boorstein, Sylvia, *It's Easier Than You Think*, HarperCollins 1995.

———, *That's Funny, You Don't Look Buddhist*, HarperCollins 1997.

Buddhadasa, Bhikkhu, *Heartwood of the Bodhi Tree*, Wisdom 1997.

Chah, Ajahn, *Food for the Heart*, Wisdom 2002.

Chopra, Deepak, *Creating Health*, Houghton Mifflin 1987.

Csikszentmihalyi, Mihalyi, *Flow*, HarperCollins 1990.

Dalai Lama, His Holiness, *The Art of Happiness*, Riverhead Books 1998.

Dhiravamsa, *The Middle Path of Life*, Blue Dolphin Publishing 1974.

———, *The Way of Non-Attachment*, Thorsons 1984.

———, *The Dynamic Way of Meditation*, Thorsons 1989.

Eknath Easwaran, *The Dhammapada*, Arkana 1986.

Epstein, Mark, *Thoughts without a Thinker*, Basic Books 1995.

———, *Going to Pieces Without Falling Apart*, Bantam 1998.

———, *Going on Being*, Broadway Books 2001.

Flickstein, Matthew, *Journey to the Centre*, Wisdom 1998.

———, *Swallowing the River Ganges*, Wisdom 2001.

Ghosananda, Venerable Mah, *Step by Step*, Parallax Press 1992.

Ginsberg, Mitchell, *The Far Shore*, Motilal Banarsidass 1996.

Goleman, Daniel, *The Meditative Mind*, Tarcher Inc. 1988.

———, *Emotional Intelligence*, Bantam 1995.

————, *Destructive Emotions*, Bantam 2003.

Goldstein, Joseph, *Insight Meditation*, Shambala 1994.

————, *The Experience of Insight*, Shambala 1996.

————, *One Dharma*, Rider 2002.

———— & Kornfield, Jack, *Seeking the Heart of Wisdom*, Shambala 1987.

Gunaratana, Venerable Henepola, *Mindfulness in Plain English*, Wisdom 1993.

————, *Eight Mindful Steps to Happiness*, Wisdom 2001.

Jackson, Peter, *Buddhadasa*, Silkworm Books 2002.

Jandamit, Helen, *The Path of Peace*, Silkworm Books 1999.

Jones, Ken, *The Social Face of Buddhism*, Wisdom 1989.

Kabat-Zinn, Jon, *Full Catastrophe Living*, Bantam Doubleday 1991.

————, *Wherever you go, there you are*, Hyperion 1994.

Khema, Ayya, *Being Nobody, Going Nowhere*, Wisdom 1987.

————, *Who Is My Self?*, Wisdom 1997.

————, *Come and See for Yourself*, Weatherhill 2002.

Kornfield, Jack, *A Path with Heart*, Bantam 1993.

————, *Living Dharma*, Shambala 1996.

————, *After the Ecstasy, the Laundry*, Bantam Books 2000.

————, *The Art of Forgiveness, Lovingkindness and Peace*, Rider 2002.

Ledi Sayadaw, *The Manuals of Buddhism*, Department of Religious Affairs, Rangoon, Burma 1981.

Levine, Stephen, *A Gradual Awakening*, Anchor Books 1979.

Mahaniranonda, Achan Naeb, *Vipassan Bhvan*, The Post Publishing Company (Bangkok) 1985.

Mahasi Sayadaw, *The Progress of Insight*, Buddhist Publication Society 1978.

Ñnamoli, Venerable, *Visuddhimagga: The Path of Purification*, Buddhist Publication Society 1956/Shambala 1976.

Narada, Venerable, *Teachings of the Buddha*, Buddhist Publication Society 1988.

Nhat Hanh, Thich, *Our Appointment with Life*, Parallax Press 1990.

————, *Breathe! You are Alive*, Parallax Press 1998.

Nyanaponika, Venerable, *The Heart of Buddhist Meditation*, Rider 1962.

————, *The Vision of Dhamma*, Rider 1986.

Pandita, Sayadaw U, *In This Very Life*, Wisdom 1992.

———, *On the Path of Freedom*, Buddhist Wisdom Centre 1995.

Piyadassi, Thera, *The Seven Factors of Purification and the Insight Knowledges*, Buddhist Publication Society 1983.

Rahula, Walpola, *What the Buddha Taught*, Haw Thai Foundation (Bangkok) 1988.

Saddhatissa, H. (translation), *The Sutta-Nipta*, Curzon Press 1985.

Salzberg, Sharon, *Lovingkindness*, Shambala 1995.

———, *A Heart as Wide as the World*, Shambala 1997.

———, *Faith*, Riverhead Books, 2002.

———, ed., *Voices of Insight*, Shambala 1999.

Santorelli, Saki, *Heal Thyself: Lessons on Mindfulness in Medicine*, Crown 1999.

Silananda, Venerable U, *The Four Foundations of Mindfulness*, Wisdom 1990.

Soma, Bhikkhu, *The Way of Mindfulness*, Buddhist Publication Society 1981.

Sumedho, Ajahn, *Mindfulness: The Path to the Deathless*, Amaravati Publications 1987.

Suzuki, Shunryu, *Zen Mind, Beginner's Mind*, Weatherhill 1970.

Thynn, Thynn, *Living Meditation, Living Insight*, Dhamma Dana Publications 1995.

Titmuss, Christopher, *Light on Enlightenment*, Shambala 1999.

———, *An Awakened Life*, Shambala 2000.

Weissman, Steve and Rosemary, *Meditation, Compassion and Lovingkindness*, Samuel Weiser 1996.

Walshe, Maurice, *The Long Discourses of the Buddha (Digha Nikaya)*, Wisdom 1987.

Watson, Gay, ed., *The Psychology of Awakening*, Rider 1999.

Welwood, John, *Toward a Psychology of Awakening*, Shambala 2000.

Yupho, Dhanit, *Vipassanabhvana*, Phra Dhammakkhanda Foundation 1988.

RECOMMENDED READING

PERIODICALS

Buddhism Now, Sharpham Coach Yard, Ashprington, Totnes TQ9
7UT, U.K. Tel. 00-44-1803-732-082, fax 00-44-1803-732-
037.Website: www.buddhismnow.com
Tricycle, in Europe represented by: Wisdom Books, 25 Stanley Road,
Ilford, Essex IG1 1RW, U.K. Tel. 00-44-20-8553-5020,
fax 00-44-20-8553-5122. Email: sales@wisdombooks.org
Website: www.wisdom-books.com

Inquiring Mind, newsletter of the *vipassana* Sangha in the U.S.
Address: P.O. Box 9999, North Berkeley Station, Berkeley, CA 94709,
U.S.A. For European subscriptions: Jean-Luc Moreau, CH-3123 Belp,
Switzerland.

AUDIO TAPES

Dharma Seed Tape Library, Box 66, Wendell Depot, MA 01380,
U.S.A. Tel. 00-1-800-969-7333.
Website: www.dharmaseed.org

Frits Koster has been practising insight meditation for about twenty-five years, and as a monk he meditated for six years in monasteries in Thailand, Burma and Sri Lanka. He subsequently disrobed, and now works as a psychiatric nurse. Apart from his work in psychiatry, he lectures in Buddhist psychology, facilitates meditation retreats at home and abroad, and offers courses in stress management and burnout prevention in the healthcare and service sector.